Story Alchemy

The Search for
the Philosopher's Stone of Storytelling

by

David Sheppard

Tragedy's Workshop
Healdsburg, CA

Copyright 2014 by David Sheppard
All rights reserved. Published in the United States
by Tragedy's Workshop, Healdsburg, CA
ISBN-13: 978-0-9910028-1-8
ISBN-10: 0-9910028-1-4

Cover illustrations and design
by Richard Sheppard
www.artstudios.com

Publisher Web site:
www.TragedysWorkshop.com

Author Web site:
www.DShep.com

Book Web site:
www.Story-Alchemy.com

Acknowledgements

Many thanks to my son Richard, who read the first draft and provided valuable suggestions. He also put up with me yakking incessantly about story, alchemy, and Jungian psychology while I was writing this.

Author's Note

I intend *Story Alchemy, The Search for the Philosopher's Stone of Storytelling* to be a companion volume to *Novelsmithing, The Structural Foundation of Plot Character and Narration.* Whereas *Novelsmithing* addresses more directly the craft of novel writing, *Story Alchemy* focuses on the inner processes of storytelling and may more readily be applied to all forms of narrative fiction and screenwriting. *Story Alchemy* bears a relationship to alchemy but is also entrenched in depth psychology. I ran onto many of the principles developed in these pages while studying and practicing modified therapeutic techniques suggested by Carl Gustav Jung. Specifically, I developed this material using Jung's Active Imagination but redirected its emphasis to better suit the needs of an author.

I have seen fit to capitalize the first letters of some words normally left lowercase. These words have a more specialized meaning in Jungian psychology as opposed to casual usage. These are words such as Consciousness, the Unconscious, the Shadow, Transcendent Function, etc.

In the last few decades, game theory has also taken on the methods of narrative storytelling, and yet it has maintained its inclination to keep the player at center stage and actively engaged in the unfolding action. For that reason, game theory has become an extremely interesting subject and hotly contested. I do have something to say about game theory, but this book didn't seem the place to express it. Instead, I've created a new blog at gamesmithing.com. I'll post my thoughts on the subject there as time and inclination permit.

The reader should realize that what I put forth here is the culmination of sixty years of reading, writing and research. This is in many ways the apex of my life's work. Although it starts out with elementary concepts, it rapidly becomes more complex, and the material more difficult to conceptualize. I've provided a number of illustrations to help get the ideas across. My hope is that the reader will visit these pages time and again to come to terms with the subject matter. In many ways, it is a psychic pilgrimage into the vast little-known world of the soul.

I would also like to reinforce the fact that all the personal experiences and dreams I convey in *Story Alchemy* actually occurred as described. I've fabricated nothing, nor have I changed the circumstance to fit the situation for a more compelling narrative.

One thing for sure. You've seen nothing like this.

Table of Contents

CHAPTER 1 The Quest	5
CHAPTER 2 Out of Chaos: The Prima Materia	13
CHAPTER 3 The Plot Pentagon	27
CHAPTER 4 Down the Rabbit Hole	47
CHAPTER 5 The Dark Realm of the Unconscious	57
CHAPTER 6 The Philosopher's Stone	67
CHAPTER 7 Becoming Worthy	80
CHAPTER 8 The Iris of Time	100
CHAPTER 9 The Land of Story	113
CHAPTER 10 Dream Invasion	131
CHAPTER 11 The Memory Palace	149
CHAPTER 12 The Vampire Novel	169
Addendum I Excerpt from Rhetorica Ad Herennium	180
Addendum II Raw Active Imagination Session	188
Bibliography	195
Index	199

Story Alchemy

The Search for
the Philosopher's Stone of Storytelling

Because many have written of the Philosopher's Stone without any knowledge of the art, and the few books extant, written by our learned predecessors and true masters hereupon, are either lost or concealed in the collections of such (however despised) as are lovers and seekers of natural secrets, we have taken a resolution to communicate our knowledge in this matter, to the intent that those who are convinced the Philosophical Work is no fiction, but grounded in the possibility of Nature, may be faithfully directed in their studies, and have an undoubted criterion to distinguish between such authors as are genuine sons of science and those who are spurious, as writing by hearsay only. —Eirenaeus Philalethes (George Starkey 1627-1665), "The Stone of the Philosophers."

CHAPTER 1 The Quest

On January 23, 2013, I woke in the middle of the night and lay in bed listening to coyotes howl outside and thinking about a new book on storytelling I was writing for which I had no title. I'd been drawn into a crazy approach involving alchemy, Jungian psychology, and mathematics by a series of coincidences, which had paid off in surprising revelations. Yet, something was missing, not in my methodology but in its characterization. The coyotes kept yelping in the forest beyond the meadow in back of our home where darkness pervaded a moonless night. I sank back into myself, almost fell asleep, and then with a flash of insight, I realized what I had done. I'd found the Philosopher's Stone of storytelling. This is the story of what led me to that discovery.

★

Such was the contention of alchemists that an element exists, called the *nigredo* [Latin for "black"] or *prima materia* [prime material], that was matter's original primitive and base state. Use of this primal substance was the first step in the long quest to obtain the Philosopher's Stone, which transmuted lead into gold and under the name Elixir of Life provided immortality. Once having obtained the prima materia, the alchemist followed detailed but coded procedures to produce, after decades of slaving over a hot, smelly furnace, the sacred Stone. Invariably, the quest ended in failure because the process had a catch. To find the correct path to the Philosopher's Stone and wield it once found, the alchemist had to be worthy. Every alchemist knew that within the dark recesses of his own inner being, a human nigredo also existed, and this Shadow of the Soul had to be transmuted as well. To become worthy, she/he had to attain personal perfection along the way.

The culmination of two thousand years of alchemy came at the hands of Sir Isaac Newton. We don't think of Newton as an alchemist, a much maligned and discredited pseudoscientific profession, but he was, having spent decades in pursuit of this "forbidden" knowledge. He was also a true scientist, and his Laws of Motion and Gravity came to govern the mechanical theories of the Universe for two hundred and fifty years until Albert Einstein's Theory of Relativity replaced them with what might be termed the Philosopher's Stone of cosmology. Even today, we have put men on the Moon and robots on Mars using Newton's Laws as an accurate and easily manageable physics that predicts motion on Earth and throughout the Solar System. Newton's Laws, obtained by decades of studying alchemy and performing rudimentary scientific research, were his Philosopher's Stone. They didn't change lead into gold, but they did turn a world of scientific chaos into a manageable, predictable arena of scientific inquiry and led directly to the Scientific Revolution.

The decades spent in pursuit of alchemical goals provided him with an acceptance of theories that involved action at a distance (gravity) and the concept of force, an invisible quantity that acted between interacting bodies to produced motion. Newton transmuted alchemy's philosophical principles into intellectual gold.

If this is true of science, one might well wonder why no one has found a Philosopher's Stone for storytelling. The reading, theatrical and movie-going public have an insatiable appetite for story, and yet so many, indeed most, writers stumble and fall in their attempts at telling a good one. Even the master storytellers

The Quest

of Hollywood puzzle over the basics, sometimes hitting the mark and at others missing so badly that they spend tens and even hundreds of millions of dollars on special effects, trying to cover up their storytelling deficiencies. They end up not with gold but fool's gold.

Writers can't even agree on how to define the key elements of storytelling. Definitions for theme, plot, and storyline are without consensus and have no actionable content. Do we have any hope of finding such a Philosopher's Stone? Who would believe that he or she had been given a truth the equivalent of Newton's Laws that could straighten out the process? Who would claim to be such an adept?

I believe such an "object" does exist. I believe we see bits and pieces of it in all the writings of those who have tried to lead us forward. Yet, storytelling is a primitive art even though it has had eloquent practitioners who have tried to convey their knowledge. Henry James, Annie Dillard, Syd Field, Irwin R. Blacker, Janet Burroway, Robert McKee, Stephen King, Richard Walter, along with many others have provided sound device on both the art and craft of writing. And yet, no specific, detailed and consistent guidance on how to plot and integrate the organic elements of character, conflict and theme exists. So the question persists: What is the underlying nature, the physics, of storytelling?

This problem didn't start yesterday. Here's a quote from Aristotle that illustrates how difficult plotting was for tragic poets back 2,400 years ago:

...beginners succeed earlier with the diction and characters than with the construction of a story; and the same may be said of nearly all the early dramatists. We maintain, therefore, that the first essential, the life and soul, so to speak, of tragedy is the plot... [Poetics, 6]

Aristotle didn't see plot as just an important part of storytelling. He called it the "life and soul" of the work. He was talking about epic poetry, tragedy, as well as comedy and dithyrambic poetry, all of which he calls "modes of imitation" of life. All storytelling is an imitation of life. But even Aristotle's advice provides nothing actionable. It doesn't help us get the words on the page.

To whom can we turn to get a surefire way to construct a story? If we follow the examples of Sir Isaac Newton and the alchemists, we could spend decades searching for such a Philosopher's Stone. Even if we found it, would we recognize it? Would we be able to wield it? The alchemists were on an outward quest for knowledge but also an inner purification of the heart to become worthy.

I started my own search some four decades ago in Denver, Colorado with my first attempt at a novel. I quit after one hundred or so pages because I didn't know where my dystopian story was going. I had a good idea, I thought, but after exploring the situation I envisioned, my story lost steam because it had no direction. It ran aground in a sea of possibilities. I tried again and again but always ran up against one stumbling block after another. In the '80s and '90s, I read about craft, took classes at the University of Colorado, formed a writing group, joined the Rocky Mountain Writers Guild, and over a period of five years, I finished my first novel, not set in a post-apocalyptic world but my own hometown. The crucial principles I learned concerned two elements of story: the premise and the central conflict. Since then, I've written and published three more novels, along with a couple of nonfiction works and a few short stories and essays. One of the books, *Novelsmithing*, is on the craft of narrative fiction.

At the same time, I was constantly reading self-help books. I was always interested in psychology, and I even briefly entered group therapy following a divorce. I kept a journal. In 1988, I entered therapy in earnest with a psychiatrist, and I continued two-a-week sessions for almost five years. Shortly afterward, on January 1, 1993, I got laid off from my day job, astronautical engineering no less. (Yes, I was a rocket scientist, and Newton's Laws of Motion and Gravity were the tools of my trade. Engineer/scientist by day, novelist/poet by night.) I decided not to return to my profession immediately and instead went on a pilgrimage to Greece where I confronted myself with the ruins of my life while visiting ancient religious sites for two and one half months. During the following two years, I turned my journal of that trip into a travel book and published it under the title *Oedipus on a Pale Horse*. I learned that narrative nonfiction contained the same story elements and structure as that for fiction.

I then decided not to return to my profession at all, but to write full time, and I moved to Carlsbad, New Mexico where I lived in an old house my grandfather had built with his own hands. Not particularly plush but certainly adequate for a struggling writer. When I ran low on funds, I went to work in the library at the local branch of New Mexico State University. In addition, I taught classes in Greek mythology, novel writing, and astronomy. I turned my class notes into my book *Novelsmithing*.

Still, I seemed to be missing something and continued my work investigating the nature of storytelling. I ran into the writings of Carl Gustav Jung, the founder of analytical psychology, who had a special interest in mythology and what it has to say about the human experience. I read many of his works and those of other Jungian psychologists, much of which surprisingly enough has to do with alchemy. Jung's last work is the massive (695 pages) *Mysterium Coniunctionis*, which contains decades of his study and reflection on philosophical alchemy, principally the synthesis of opposites. This "synthesis" to me implied the resolution of conflict and led me to develop a new theory of storytelling.

Then in mid June 2009, I made a breakthrough in my research. In the ensuing days, I extended this new theory. For four years, this investigation kept expanding, but the full importance of the discovery eluded me. I didn't fully realize what I had uncovered until the morning of January 23, 2013 when it came to me in a flash. I realized that I had finally discovered the Philosopher's Stone.

In the following chapters, I provide directions for creating this magic "object." It took me forty years of hard labor to learn the true nature of the writing process and decode it. What I am offering you is the inside story on the nature of storytelling. Even

Story Alchemy

if I do give you the Philosopher's Stone, will you be able to wield it? In the words of the alchemists, "Are you worthy?" Probably not. Jung cites an old Chinese proverb: "If the wrong man uses the right means, the right means work in the wrong way." [*Alchemical Studies*, page 7]

Don't lose heart. I also know something about remedying this worthiness issue. Jung's method of individuation, much of which he developed while studying the alchemists, could well get you there. The good news is that the process of writing fiction, at least the method I'll provide, is an offshoot of the path to individuation so that while practicing your craft, you are also traveling the road to becoming worthy. Just as the ancient alchemist perfected himself by looking within while practicing his alchemy, so will your writing efforts, if done properly, serve a dual purpose. By staying on the right path to good storytelling, you become worthy.

Here's a word of caution. Sir Isaac Newton may have found the Philosopher's Stone for physics, but he paid a price. He had an emotional collapse and almost didn't survive the process. Plus, he was a different person once he came out the other side. He was no longer much of a scientist and became a bureaucrat. Unaccountably, he accepted an appointment to be Warden of the Royal Mint. No one remains unaffected by a process that looks so deep into the psyche. You might have a good talk with yourself concerning your own emotional stability before getting into what I'm going to present here. I'll have more to say on this as we proceed.

★

On May 22, 2010 while practicing a visualization technique with my eyes closed, I noticed a light patch in the psychic darkness and focused on it. It immediately exposed the tips of three mountains outlined by the bright light coming from behind. I continued to focus on this image, trying to get it to expand into something meaningful, when the image split and became dynamic. The background light consolidated into a brilliant ball, and the dark mountains became a black ball. Both started moving about my

The Quest

field of view and then circled like heavenly bodies orbiting each other, each growing a tail and appearing comet-like. Their orbital motion decreased in radii until they were practically touching. And then they stopped. I made a rough sketch of these psychic images with colored pencils, and the result is shown in Figure 1-1.

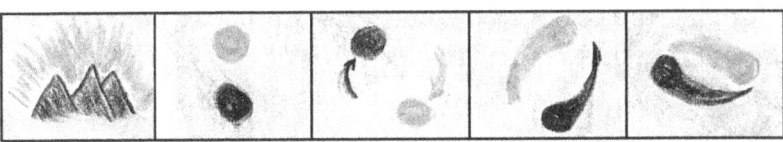

Figure 1-1 Psychic Derivation of Yin-Yang Symbol

While all this was happening, I was a passive observer. I didn't know what would happen from second to second, as if I were watching an animation. When it finished, I recognized it as the yin-yang from Chinese alchemy. I had seen the symbol derived before my eyes. I also realized that it was similar to the symbol for Cancer, my astrological sign. I thought that the little light's shenanigans were remarkable but didn't pursue the subject further.

Then on September 11, 2010, I ran across the yin-yang symbol on the Internet and learned that yin (shade) can represent the shaded north-side of a mountain and yang (sunny) can represent the Sun. It would seem that initially I was positioned on the opposite side of the mountain range relative to the Sun, which was either rising or setting. The yin and yang relationship is often described as sunlight over a mountain and in a valley, which of course was my initial vision.

I was astonished that this symbol had appeared spontaneously and with many of the attributes used to describe it through the millennia. It is a universal concept that conveys the interconnectedness and dependency of contrary forces. They give birth to each other. Although we generally think of the symbol as originating with Chinese alchemy, it is also a part of Celtic, Etruscan, and Roman iconography and goes back possibly three thousand years.

My psychic event occurred three days after I started visualization as a part of writing *Story Alchemy*. I'll have much more to say about this technique, particularly in Chapter 7. This was one of several episodes that led me to believe that a real adventure awaited me. I wasn't disappointed. You won't be either.

★

This is where I'll leave off this introductory chapter and start providing the details of my quest. Is it an unraveling of a strict scientific discipline? Hardly.

We tend to think of theory development as emerging out of an objective, scientific attitude. Wrong. All theory is autobiography. The person the theorist really wants to understand, more than anyone, is himself. The subjective can never be elbowed aside. It hovers inescapably, like an off-stage voice, whispering, whispering, whispering... [William Todd Schultz, Ph.D., "Why Freud and Jung Broke Up," *Psychology Today* in Genius and Madness, May 19, 2009]

Of necessity, this is a personal narrative about an intimate creative process. Have I truly found a Philosopher's Stone for all storytellers? You'll have to decide for yourself.

CHAPTER 2 Out of Chaos: The Prima Materia

Undoubtedly, the beginning of story creation comes with the author's idea for a writing project. In alchemical terms, this is the prima materia, the primitive formless state of all matter and the seed of enlightenment — the original material from the origin of the universe, so to speak. But how would an author know a good idea, one that can be developed into a full story, when she/he found it? Here's what Jung had to say about this beginning state for the alchemist:

> For him there was first of all an initial state in which opposite tendencies or forces were in conflict; secondly there was the great question of a procedure which would be capable of bringing the hostile elements and qualities, once they were separated, back to unity again. The initial state, named the chaos, was not given from the start but had to be sought for as the prima materia. And just as the beginning of the work was not self-evident, so to an even greater degree was its end. [*Mysterium Coniunctionis* xiv]

If we didn't know better, we could mistake this for the initial step in storytelling. The second part of this statement tells us, by analogy, that the idea comes from the "chaos" of one's internal psychic state. It may be triggered by an external event or just pop into one's mind out of nowhere. It may even come to mind from a thoughtful search of newspaper headlines that emotionally resonate. Jung has given another clue in the first part of the paragraph: "opposite tendencies or forces were in conflict." It can come to the author as an unusual scene, exotic setting, or an intriguing character. Regardless of the source, for it to qualify as a good idea for a story, it must at least have the possibility of opposing forces, i.e., animated characters with clashing wills. This requirement is actionable in that we know we must have conflict.

Is conflict as necessary for storytelling as it was for Alchemy? Syd Field says:

All drama is conflict. Without conflict you have no character; without character, you have no action; without action you have no story. [*Screenplay*, page 12]

That pretty well settles the issue. When you take away conflict, the entire story doesn't just fall flat. It disappears entirely. It loses its sense of foreshadowing. The reader responds to conflict with anticipation.

But what if the idea doesn't seem to have conflict? This doesn't necessarily mean that it is an inferior idea. It may simply mean that the conflict is subtler than one would expect. Stories that start out like this can end up being some of the more profound. If this is true, then the author must apply something to separate the subject matter and develop, as Jung stated, its "opposite tendencies or forces."

The way to come into closer contact with your idea is to close your eyes and see it as an image. It may well be impossible for an idea for a story to form in the mind without images. After mentally picturing your idea, concentrate on it. The mere act of contemplating should cause it to animate. Follow the movement wherever it takes you but continually look for evidence of conflict. Perhaps other characters will pop into view, and you can see how they come into disagreement. In this way, you should be able to envision what the conflict is over. You should also be able to better define your characters after witnessing them in this

Out of Chaos: The Prima Materia

context.

This is the prima materia.

I practiced this little exercise to come up with an example. What immediately came to mind was a US Civil War soldier conflicted over whether to fight and if so, for which side. This idea had its origin in a story my mother used to tell. She had an uncle who lived on the Mason-Dixon Line, and although he did own a few slaves to work his fields viewed himself as a part of the North rather than the Confederacy. The image I had that took on the form of prima materia was of him running with a shotgun to the cane break to hide as Confederacy soldiers came to force him into service.

You may find that this little visualizing exercise will work better in the evening just before sleep or during the night when you wake. It also may be approached in the early morning just after you wake but before getting out of bed. Any time will work actually, but these times seem to produce the best results. In a later chapter, I'll provide more detail on this technique. For now, trust the process and your ability to activate your imagination through animating psychic images. What is crucial in all this is that the idea must be your own and something that intrigues you. This conflict must come from within you, and interest in it then is the reason you've selected it above all other possibilities. This "affinity" will have implications downstream. Without that personal connection, it's doubtful that the idea has the relationship to you and your psychological makeup so important during the difficult task of imagining the material to flesh out the story. To be "intrigued" by an idea is to see its possibilities and be willing to put in the work necessary to fulfill its potential. Creative writing is an exceptionally sticky subject. Just when you think you've succeeded in getting the story "out there" and "away" from you, after all it is about other people, you learn that it has crept up behind you and somehow attached itself to your backside, or perhaps your underbelly.

Assuming the idea has your approval, you're ready to take a

closer look. You should be able to intuit the nature of the conflict and put it into a more useful form. Don't be deluded by thinking that it should be an all out, no-holds-barred conflict to the death. Some conflict is like that, but it isn't always or even generally true. Conflict isn't even necessarily hostile. Conflict between two friends or family members can be over something each views as being in the best interest of the other party. Conflict within this context is a multi-sided phenomenon and one well worth studying, so invest a little more time in understanding the essence of conflict.

Unmotivated conflict can be irritating for the reader, and conflict for conflict's sake isn't what we're after. And yet it frequently happens, particularly in television series episodes. Here is how I believe the source of the problem came about, and it comes from one of our most brilliant teachers. Richard Walter is a professor and screenwriting chairman at UCLA. Here's how he introduces the subject matter for Chapter 5 "Conflict: Violence and Sex" in his highly acclaimed book *Essentials of Screenwriting, The Art, Craft, and Business of Film and Television Writing*:

Must movies marinate in sex? Must they wallow in violence?

No, but many, probably most — including some of the finest films ever made — are positively saturated with sensuality and eroticism. Likewise, worthy movies must forever be violent.

If you prefer, you may think of violence as conflict or tension or stress. Screenwriters are urgently advised to consider the general disquietude essential to film as full-tilt, mean-spirited, straight-ahead violence. I urge them also to remember that enlightened, reasonable, rational discourse and courtesy, consideration, and consensus occupy an important place in our lives. In movies, however, they're boring.

I don't suggest that movie armies must perpetually beat out each other's brains, nor that all good films must provide an endless succession of looting, shooting, and rape. Neither do I hold that all movies must be greasy, oily sex orgies. All the same, however, emotional unrest must be integrated into each and every frame of each and every scene of each and every movie. [page 48]

Out of Chaos: The Prima Materia

Something is wrong in Movieville, and this is it. The last two sentences in the next to last paragraph, "I urge them ... they're boring" is what I object to. Granted you can't build a story off of courtesy, consideration, and consensus but you can use it to build likable bonded characters. If you don't, you'll have hateful, mean-spirited, unsympathetic characters no one will care about. Not only that. Conflicts that follow what those two sentences tell us are banal, superficial and can totally ruin a storyline.

Take a movie like *The Perks of Being a Wallflower* (2012) and remove three scenes: (1) where Charlie is welcomed into his little band of misfits, (2) where Charlie gets kissed by Sam (Emma Watson), and (3) Sam in the back of the pickup with her arms in the air like she's flying while David Bowie blares over the radio "We Could Be Heroes." Without those scenes, which have no conflict, the movie wouldn't capture the viewers' love for the characters.

I want to go a little deeper into that scene where Sam kisses Charlie. A little background. Charlie, as a freshman who is emotionally disturbed and struggling, has never kissed a girl. But Sam, a senior, had her virginity taken when she was fourteen by her father's business partner, and she has felt degraded and not worthy of someone nice ever since. Sam doesn't want Charlie to have a bad experience the first time he kisses a girl. Sam tells Charlie that she wants the first person to kiss him to be someone who loves him. She sets him down on her bed, puts her arms around him and kisses him. She then tells him that she loves him, and he tells her that he loves her too.

This scene is so beautifully setup and executed that it just melts your heart. It does carry the "emotional unrest" of which Richard Walter speaks in his last sentence, and this comes about because of both characters' previous traumatic experiences. People caring for each other and acting in their friends' best interests is not something to avoid but something to exploit and is too frequently overlooked. Some of these master storytellers feel immune to criticism by virtue of their professional position.

Story Alchemy

But Richard Walter is wrong about this.

Another good example is the recently cancelled series on the SyFy channel titled *Caprica* (2009-10). As a prequel to the highly successful *Battlestar Galactica* as re-envisioned by Ron Moore and Remi Aubuchon, it had an eager viewership from the beginning, and it appeared to be on its way to hitdom when SyFy presented the pilot. But as the story developed, all the characters deteriorated into mean, evil people without a sympathetic side. Though the series was steeped in conflict, few viewers wanted to watch it. High ratings for the pilot plummeted when the series hit its stride and viewers saw how ill-conceived the characters and plot were. Conflict is a necessary ingredient but not a panacea.

One last example. Pixar had a near fumble with the development of *Toy Story*. And this illustrates that conflict with its many ramifications and character implications can make or break a story. It should be ever-present, but at the same time, it can destroy the story if it doesn't fit both the proper mood and the characters it engages. Walter Isaacson in his biography of Steve Jobs talks about Pixar's near miss when it allowed Disney to get involved in the evolution of *Toy Story*. The big problem was Jeffrey Katzenberg, the head of Disney's film division at the time.

> *The two main characters went through many iterations before they ended up as Buzz Lightyear and Woody. Every couple of weeks, Lasseter and his team would put together their latest set of storyboards or footage to show the folks at Disney. ... At each presentation by Pixar, Katzenberg would tear much of it up, barking out his detailed comments and notes. And a cadre of clipboard-carrying flunkies was on hand to make sure every suggestion and whim uttered by Katzenberg received follow-up treatment.*
>
> *Katzenberg's big push was to add more edginess to the two main characters. ...he kept pushing for what he called "edge," and that meant making Woody's character more jealous, mean, and belligerent toward Buzz, the new interloper in the toy box. "It's a toy-eat-toy world," Woody says at one point, after pushing Buzz out of a window.*
>
> *After many rounds of notes from Katzenberg and other Disney execs, Woody had been stripped of almost all charm. ... As Tom Hanks, who*

Out of Chaos: The Prima Materia

had signed up to be Woody's voice, exclaimed at one point, "This guy's a real jerk!" [Jobs, page 286/7]

The story and characters were in such a mess that Disney stopped production. Lasseter talked Disney into letting him take *Toy Story* back to Pixar to be reworked. They took the "edge" off the characters, made them work together, and produced an endearing story, satisfying to both children and adults. Steve Jobs had to use personal funding to keep the project going because of the rework. When it was finally released:

...*Toy Story* opened to blockbuster commercial and critical success. It recouped its cost the first weekend, with a domestic opening of $30 million, and it went on to becoming the top-grossing film of the year... [Jobs, page 290]

What I wish to point out is that continuous, mean-spirited conflict is always reflected in the characters, and this may sell a story to a studio, but it's not what sells a story to its audience. And yet, the statement that "in fiction, the only thing of interest is conflict" contains more than a grain of truth. But mean-spirited conflict can destroy characters, as Pixar learned with Woody, and other avenues of developing conflict must be explored to allow character bonding. Sometimes characters are in conflict over their concern for each other.

For an example of this, let's take look at a single scene from *Buffy the Vampire Slayer* that, although steeped in conflict, is irresistible viewing. The scene I'm thinking of comes at the end of Season 5, the very last episode. Buffy has been battling a god, Glory, who is trapped [Glory-OtherGods conflict] in a human body and practically invincible. Although in the scene I have in mind, Buffy has defeated Glory [Buffy-Glory conflict], Glory has captured Dawn, Buffy's sister, [Glory-Dawn conflict] and has her held at the top of a tower where an instability in the fabric of the universe has occurred. Dawn's blood will open a passageway between this reality and the demon dimension that will cause them to merge and subject human beings to immeasurable suffering [Human-Demons conflict]. When Buffy gets to the top of the tower, she finds that Dawn has already been bled and that drops of her blood have already opened the crack between worlds through which demons are now streaming. The only way Buffy can close the crack is to stop the flow of Dawn's blood by killing her [Buffy-Dawn conflict]. This is something Buffy refuses to do [Buffy-Buffy conflict]. She's already told Giles, her Watcher, that if Dawn has to die, she's through being a Slayer [Buffy-Calling conflict], and that if anyone tries to hurt Dawn, including Giles himself and her friends, Xander, Willow, or Anya, she'll kill them [Slayer-Watcher conflict, Buffy-friends conflict].

The two girls stand there at the top of the tower, and Dawn, realizing that she has to die to stop the influx of demons [Dawn-Demons conflict], tells Buffy that she (Dawn) has to jump. But Buffy won't let her [Dawn-Buffy conflict]. At this point, Buffy doesn't care about the world or anything in it, if those are the choices [Buffy-Reality conflict]. She stops Dawn from jumping.

Then Buffy remembers something she was told by the First Slayer: "Death is your gift." Buffy also realizes that Dawn was made from her [can't really get into that] and that Dawn's blood and her blood are the same. Dawn doesn't have to die, if Buffy dies. Death is her gift, not only to Dawn, but to the world.

When Buffy realizes this, Dawn can see it in her eyes and tells Buffy no. She won't let Buffy die in her place [new Buffy-Dawn conflict]. But Buffy explains to Dawn that this is her [Buffy's] calling, that this is her job. She has to do it. And in true heroic fashion, Buffy is so pleased, because now it all makes sense. Her life is not meaningless. She can give it to save Dawn and the World. She tells Dawn that she loves her, that she will always love her, and to be brave, that the most difficult thing in the world is to live it. Then she turns, makes the short run along the ramp, and jumps into the crack between worlds. We get one last view of her, her face as she goes down, grim with determination to do this as she's always done her Slayer duties: giving it everything she has within her, waging her war with every ounce of energy.

Out of Chaos: The Prima Materia

It took giving her life, but Buffy saved the World, again.

This scene is so steeped in conflict that hardly a word or an action isn't a reaction to some form of conflict. And yet, the two girls each have a chance to stand up for each other, to fight for each other's survival, each to try to prevent the other from dying, and all while saying they love each other.

This is a scene to rip your heart out. The tears shed by Buffy fans because of this one scene would fill an ocean. But you don't feel mad, drained, or beat up. You feel uplifted, loved, amazed that we have such a hero. Conflict, along with courtesy and consideration, has done its job, again.

The point I'm making is that story conflict isn't always a character looking out for their own wellbeing nor is it necessarily mean-spirited with everyone hating each other. Conflict has many facets, and the storyteller should be a student of the art of opposing wills. Richard Walter is wrong. Enlightened, reasonable, rational discourse and courtesy, consideration, and consensus are not necessarily boring. If you don't believe in them, you will make them boring, but if you are talented and have your heart in the right place, you can use these concepts to make your story irresistible. Let me turn this is into a general rule, an axiom that you can trust:

Any aspect of human nature and social interaction, when used properly, can be valuable and may even be indispensable in telling your story.

Of course, the real problem is that — and I believe this is what Richard Walter is reacting against, and reasonably so — we live life with the softer elements of social discourse ingrained in us. They are the behaviors we have adopted to become civilized. Most movies, most stories really, are not about the civilized. Something like George Clooney's *The Descendants* and Robert Bendton's *Kramer vs. Kramer* belie this, even though the stories are deeply dependent on conflict. But most first-time storytellers won't have the skill to execute a worthwhile story if they don't concentrate on the sorrier side of humanity. We'll address this issue and why it's necessary at times to expose humanity's underbelly rather indiscriminately, as well as its pitfalls, in Chapter 5.

Another thing to realize is that a relationship exists between these people who are in conflict, the protagonist and antagonist. In many ways, they are mirror images of each other. Just as you, the author, have an affinity for the conflict you're making into a story, these characters lock up because they feel strongly about something they have in common. They are the two components of a yin-yang relationship. They interrelate and give rise to each other as primary characters. This is very much in keeping with the symbol I uncovered with my visualization technique I described in Chapter 1.

Not all conflicts are external to the protagonist, i.e., directed at someone else. Many conflicts, some of the more intriguing actually, are internal. The protagonist is "conflicted" about something. A woman may have a desire to have a child but still be apprehensive of how it might affect her career. When she approaches forty, she can hear her biological clock ticking and feel the pressure to make a decision. It could be the Civil War soldier mentioned earlier, who may be internally conflicted about killing people, even the enemy. Internal conflicts are just as interesting and multi-faceted as are external conflicts, and they all have a protagonist and an antagonist. The internal conflict just has staked out opposite sides of the character's psyche.

Another aspect of practically all conflict between individuals is that it may well be a metaphor for a higher-level conflict, i.e., the individual may represent the universal. The protagonist may be the symbol of good and the antagonist the symbol of evil. Think Luke Skywalker versus Darth Vader. Some writers will tell you that all stories ultimately come down to good versus evil. This black-and-white world can be simplistic and not intellectually challenging. Look for philosophical nuance within the cast of characters. Your protagonist may also have flaws, and your antagonist some endearing characteristics.

Out of Chaos: The Prima Materia

★

Now we'll take a quick look at what some of the most influential writers have to say about this initial story idea. We'll draw from what the most accomplished storytellers and educators tell us, particularly those from the world of cinema where the pressure to produce good structured stories is most intense.

Both Lajos Egri, a playwright and teacher, and Erwin R. Blacker, a screenwriter and professor, tell us that we must transform the idea into what they call a premise. Blacker says, "The premise is the basis of the conflict." [*The Elements of Screenwriting*, page 6] Egri says that the foundation of a story is built on a premise that has three parts, and those parts reflect character, conflict and conclusion. In other words, you need to know both the beginning and ending of your story. Egri gives an example: "Frugality leads to waste." He says "frugality" implies character, "leads to" implies conflict, and "waste" implies the ending [*The Art of Dramatic Writing*, page 8]. I don't see how "leads to" necessarily implies conflict, and I'll take a somewhat different approach.

The basic formulation of all conflict is: protagonist versus antagonist, which implies conflict between opposing wills. The premise then might be expressed as: "Protagonist overcomes Antagonist." Both characters show up in this presentation of the premise, and the word "overcomes" implies both conflict and the outcome. In this example, the protagonist rules, although the opposite result would be equally valid for a story. Egri's formulation has the advantage of containing thematic material. "Frugality" and "waste" point to subject matter and character attributes that take the premise out of the generic realm and into real-world concerns, and as such, the story starts to take on meaning, and that meaning is a result of the theme.

Imagine my Civil War soldier who grew up on the Mason-Dixon Line and had family members on both sides, some siblings fighting for the North and others for the South. With the war as the background conflict, this story would have several levels, each governed by a separate premise. The man could not only be fighting for the South, but wondering if he should be fighting for the North and also arguing with his wife and kids over the same issue. What we should learn from this is that a premise can work at different levels, even within the same story. Here are some possibilities, framed only in terms of conflict:

>Opposing Countries: America versus the Confederacy
>Opposing Cities: Washington DC versus Atlanta, GA
>Opposing Families: North Family versus South Family
>Opposing Siblings: Brother versus Brother
>Opposing Family Members: Wife versus Husband
>Soldier Internal Conflict: Join North versus Join South

One story could, and in this case should, have all these levels of conflict. As a matter of fact, it's next to impossible to tell a story that doesn't at least imply several levels of conflict. Another thing you might notice about all these examples is that the identification of the protagonist and antagonist depends on perspective. One man's hero is another's enemy.

Of course, these formulations do not address the nature of the conflict, what it's about. Many experts who teach storytelling fail to understand that the essence of the conflict is the theme of the story and says everything about character. Those who do not have a vested interest in the story they are telling frequently don't get this. If all we talk about is the North at war with the South, we have opposing wills and the soldiers will definitely kill each other, but why? If we don't address the theme, along with the conflict, that has brought these armies together, we have a story without a soul. It's meaningless. In many ways, conflict is a mechanism for exploring theme. Here are two formulations that deal directly with theme for this Civil War story:

>Opposing Cosmic Forces: Good versus Evil
>Opposing Issues: Freedom versus Slavery

The conflict involving "good" versus "evil" gives the story a cosmic scope, and once slavery is mentioned, it flavors everything

Out of Chaos: The Prima Materia

because it concerns the philosophical differences that cause the central conflict and sub-conflicts clustering about it. This is theme, the narrative's unifying subject, and it leads directly to character development. But none of these are actually a premise. Here are two possibilities for the premise:

Good overcomes Evil
Freedom overcomes Slavery

These formulations in addition to indicating conflict also address the result, i.e., they take a position relative to the outcome of the story. With Egri's and Blacker's formulation, a premise for Tolkien's *The Lord of the Rings* might be "Quest [Sauron] for absolute power leads to Destruction." In my formulation, the premise could be stated as "Evil Immortal succumbs to Hobbit." Or on a character level, "Sauron defeated by Frodo." The basic idea behind *The Lord of the Rings* is that absolute power can only be safely put in the hands of those who do not wish to have it. In this perception of story, the subject of the central conflict is the theme. And in the case of *The Lord of the Rings*, the theme concerns the nature of power. The nature of the central conflict constitutes the underlying philosophy of the story, the intellectual content that constitutes meaning.

Let's state it again: Conflict is a mechanism for exploring theme. And theme is the unifying idea behind the story. Graphically, that mechanism looks like this:

```
                        (conflict)
    Protagonist ─────────▶ Versus ◀───────── Antagonist
                     (theme – meaning)
```

Figure 2-1 Premise

Nothing I say could overemphasize the importance of understanding the nature of the central conflict. This is the basic theme of the story, and a firm grasp of it will allow you to instill meaning through characterization. We'll address this issue further in Chapter 5.

Story Alchemy

To help understand what theme is, I'll list as many as I can think of right now: slavery, greed, power, love, compassion, forbidden love, abortion, global warming, capital punishment, euthanasia, assisted suicide, betrayal, rape, murder, terrorism, war, religion, education, unemployment, human dignity, hunger, arrogance, vengeance, loyalty, etc., etc., etc. Themes speak to the human condition and unify the subject matter. Conflict puts the protagonist and antagonist under stress and reveals their strengths and weaknesses relative to the theme.

Now that you have established the prima materia, know what your story is about and that it is meaningful, you need to go a step further and plot your overall storyline.

CHAPTER 3 The Plot Pentagon

Aristotle:

...let us now consider the proper construction of the plot, as that is at once the first and the most important thing in tragedy. We have laid it down that a tragedy is an imitation of an action that is complete in itself, as a whole of some magnitude... Now a whole is that which has beginning, middle, and end. A beginning is that which is not itself necessarily after anything else, and which has naturally something else after it; an end is that which is naturally after something itself, either as its necessary or usual consequent, and with nothing else after it; and a middle, that which is by nature after one thing and has also another after it. A well-constructed plot therefore, cannot either begin or end at any point one likes; beginning and end in it must be of the forms just described. [*Poetics* 7]

As a general statement, that is hard to argue with, and we will certainly use the "beginning, middle, and end" bit. Remember that Aristotle also said, "the life and soul" of story "is the plot." Aristotle goes on to define plot as "...the combination of the incidents, or things done in the story," [*Poetics* 6] which is so vague that it's no help at all. Something is missing. We need precise directions. Something actionable.

And yet nothing is forthcoming. We get all sorts of strange

Story Alchemy

advice on how to plot a story. Jon Franklin, a two-time Pulitzer Prize winner, in *Writing for Story* says:

A story consists of a sequence of actions that occur when a sympathetic character encounters a complicating situation that he confronts and solves. [page 71]

Okay, not brilliant but still good advice. It tells us that we should have someone we care about and what should happen at the beginning and end. The problem, of course, is that a "complicating situation" can be anything and isn't actionable. It's a vague term that may have nothing to do with conflict. Advanced calculus is complicated, but it has nothing to do with conflict.

Others will tell you that after you've set up the initial situation, simply ask: What comes next? This also is not necessarily directly related to conflict. It leads to episodic storylines devoid of cause and effect. Aristotle says this about that:

Of simple plots and actions the episodic are the worst. I call a plot episodic when there is neither probability nor necessity in the sequence of its episodes. Actions of this sort bad poets construct through their own fault, and good ones on account of the players. His work being for public performance, a good poet often stretches out a plot beyond its capabilities, and is thus obliged to twist the sequence of incident. [*Poetics* 8]

If the central conflict generates the "sequence of episodes," they do have "probability" and "necessity," which clearly satisfies our requirement of having a certain inevitability, or as I term it, cause and effect. Also, since story is about conflict, until it occurs nothing is worth stating, and when it ends, nothing else is worth telling — all this in keeping with Aristotle's definition of the beginning and ending. So we need something that tells us more about the central conflict, and perhaps it should be true of all conflict.

Syd Field, one of our more successful screenwriters, further structures Aristotle's three-act play by defining two primary events he calls plot points. The first occurs 1/4 way through the story, which is: "a dramatic and unanticipated escalation in the

The Plot Pentagon

conflict." In the movie *Groundhog Day*, this is that first morning when Phil learns that Groundhog Day is repeating. We realize that Phil is not pleased with himself, and it becomes obvious that he is going to relive Groundhog Day until he changes and gets it right. It's an internal conflict that's resolved at the end.

Syd Field's second plot point occurs 3/4 of the way through the story, but he lets this milestone go undefined. I will term this plot point, "The Agony of Choice," and define it as, "the particular time where the protagonist has to make a difficult decision that will determine his/her fate."

Using Syd Field's suggestions, we break up the story much the same as Aristotle suggested, into three sections, like this:

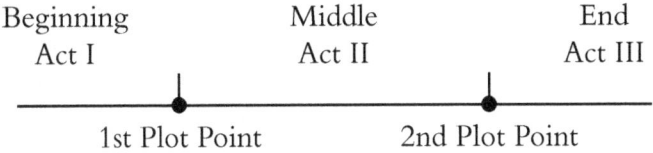

Figure 3-1 Storyline Structure - Aristotle/Field

To add more definition to the storyline, we'll turn again to Irwin R. Blacker. Everyone appears to realize that story involves conflict, but they seem to say just throw conflict at it and where it sticks, use it. We would like to have something a little more insightful, and Blacker is one of the few who provides definite instructions concerning conflict. According to him, the first thing your story should do is "lock the conflict." The protagonist and antagonist must engage in conflict, however remotely, for the story to begin. In police procedurals as either TV episodes or movies, in the initial scene, someone finds a body. If the murderer is still standing at the scene and gives up, there is no story. If the murderer runs, this act locks his/her conflict with the police. This then is the battle that will continue throughout the story and be resolved at the end when the police catch the murderer. It bounds our story. We now know how to begin and end a story: lock the conflict, resolve the conflict. This of course implies a central conflict that provides the story arc.

Story Alchemy

I will add another plot point right in the middle of the story. This comes, not from any advice from some internationally famous storyteller, but from a professor I had at the University of Colorado where I was taking classes in American literature in the late 1970s. I verified it with decades of my own research. It is a reversal in the action, i.e., the central conflict, and it occurs at the midpoint in the story. As a rather simplistic example, if the protagonist has been chasing the antagonist up to this point, then the antagonist will start chasing the protagonist afterward.

You can see this reversal in novels as well as movies. While reading James Fenimore Cooper's *The Last of the Mohicans*, my professor pointed out that the Indians chase the white guys for the first half on the novel, and the white guys chase the Indians in the second half. I then noticed that in Spielberg's *Jaws*, the fish chases the people for the first half of the film, and the people chase the fish during the second half. Twenty years later, I realized that in Cameron's *Titanic*, the ship floats during the first half and sinks during the second half. This is also where Rose decides to abandon her mother and fiancé and go with Jack. As a matter of fact, during the first half of the film, Cameron shows us every thing about Titanic. We have a long excursion on deck, and even go down into the engine room. In a sense, he is putting Titanic together, building it. Then, right in the middle of the film, Titanic hits an iceberg, and during the second half, Cameron tears it apart and sinks it.

The reversal should occur naturally and not be something you have to force on your story. It is the nature of storytelling, thus the nature of conflict. Which then dictates that Cinderella chase the prince in the first half of the story, and the prince chase her in the second half. If the reversal doesn't intuitively show up in your story structure, you might question how well you know your story. No one talks about the mid-point reversal, but it happens in all well-told stories, otherwise the conflict wouldn't be balanced or fully explored.

I would add two more minor events to our plotting technique.

The Plot Pentagon

First is the initial setup, which should be quite short. It's what precedes locking the conflict — maybe getting to know the protagonist and/or the antagonist a little before the action starts. The other thing is the denouement. That's what comes after the resolution of the conflict and shows the aftermath of the conflict. Again, very short.

When we renumber our plot points, the storyline as an evolution of the central conflict looks like Figure 3-2.

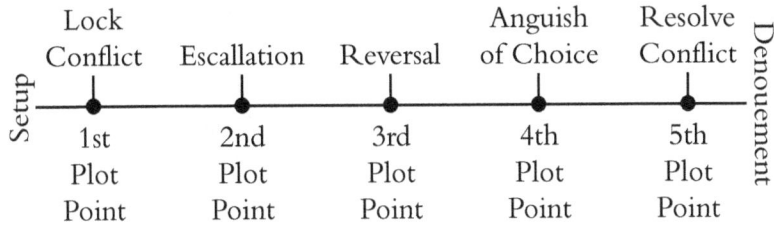

Figure 3-2 Composite Storyline Structure

This graphical representation looks appealing and has all the components mentioned by master storytellers from 400 BC up until today. This constitutes a complete idea for a story, and unless it has all these components, including the premise, the concept is incomplete. The author explores her/his idea for a story using this plot diagram as a guide to uncover its inherent structure.

We need to look a little closer at Plot Points 2 and 4. PP2 is the time in the story where both the central conflict and therefore also the theme are fully exposed. Theme and conflict are always inexorably intertwined. In *Titanic*, PP2 is when Jack asks Rose why she thinks suicide is her only way out of the shackles imposed upon her by her family. Freedom is an option, he tells her. PP4 reveals something about the theme that gives a clue to the outcome. This is usually the point where the protagonist solves the riddle of how the theme specifically applies to him/her. It involves agony of choice. In *Titanic*, this is where Rose climbs out of the lifeboat and goes back to get Jack. She's decided to go with him because he advocates a life of freedom. He and the lifestyle he offers are more important to her than family and friends, and even her own life. PP2 and PP4 say more about the theme associated with the central conflict than any other events in the story.

Before we proceed, I should say a few words about why stories should generally have this structure. The answer comes from the basic nature of conflict and the requirement that it be sustained for a prolonged period of time for it to be interesting. Conflict may well be the central element of life on Earth. Its most basic manifestation comes from the need to feed. Life forms eat each other. From there conflict spreads out to what is in the best interest in the individual and then the community in which we live. Through the millennia, this is the form that human conflict has taken on in the average. This structure for conflict is the graven riverbed humanity has traveled down through the ages.

Some call the straight-line plot of Figure 3-2 the "iron bar" that you drive through your story. It does have actionable components and is directly character-related, but it also has a rather pedestrian quality, and we're not looking for just any old plotting method. We're looking for something exceptional to illustrate the procedure. This alchemical-like activity needs a concrete symbol to give our method added meaning in the world of storytelling. Alchemists were big on symbols and when their magnum opus involved twelve procedures, they used symbols from the Zodiac. We have five "procedures" and would like to convert our iron bar into something symbolic of our process. In short, we would like to transform this linear diagram into a symbol, the study of which would reveal more of the secrets behind the art and craft of storytelling, the alchemy, something that alludes to or even captures the mysticism of conjuring the activities of fictional beings.

To get there, we're going to have to perform a little alchemy on our plot diagram, and this step requires some faith and inspired thinking. So put on your alchemist robe, tiara and leather sandals, etc. What I'm going to suggest we do with our storyline, this iron bar, is to pick it up and bend it until it forms a complete circle.

The Plot Pentagon

This might require a little heat in the alchemist's furnace, pumping the bellows, and pounding on an anvil to join the ends where the setup and denouement meet. We then have a two-dimensional circular representation of our storyline that looks like Figure 3-3.

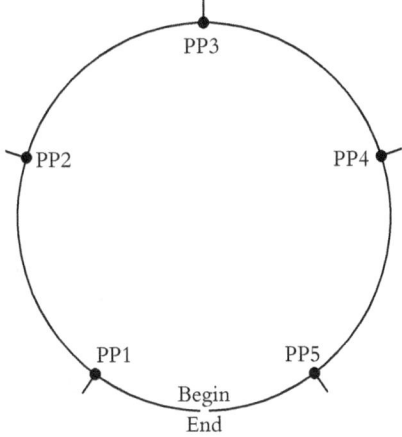

Figure 3-3 Circular Storyline

Now let's take it a step further by connecting the dots, i.e., connect the plot points with straight lines, starting with the one that represents locking the conflict, PP1, and continue around the storyline in this manner until we have connected "locking the conflict" with "resolving the conflict." Since both the "setup" and "denouement" are short, they will form one line together.

Now we have something far from pedestrian, a five-sided geometrical figure called a pentagon. See Figure 3-4. We navigate the pentagon clockwise when telling the story. The plot pentagon is not so much a diagram as a geometric object and symbol that represents not just one but all stories. It represents the most basic underlying structure of storytelling. The plot pentagon is composed of actionable elements because it is directly related to the conflict at the center of the story.

That's a profound statement and a lot to grasp all at once. We have uncovered, one might actually say discovered, the basic form of plotting. The pieces of an emerging archetype that presented themselves as plot points identified by master storytellers over a period of 2,400 years have coalesced into the defining structure that symbolizes story structure.

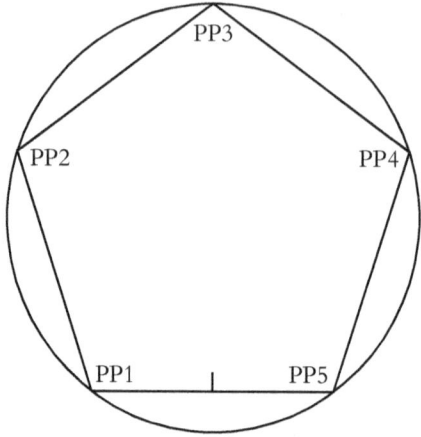

Figure 3-4 Pentagonal Storyline

Just as Sir Isaac Newton formulated his three Laws of Motion, we now know the basic structure of storytelling. This symbol represents the energy inherent in a well-told story. And notice that we haven't positioned the premise anywhere on the plot diagram. That's because it is never mentioned specifically in the story even though it influences every point along the circle and in particular every plot point. That doesn't mean that we won't talk about the theme of the story from time to time, but it does mean that we won't address this philosophical underpinning including the outcome overtly. We'll find the proper place for the premise within our plot pentagon, and it plainly does have one, in just a moment.

The bottom of the pentagon, the side that sits on the ground, so to speak, has its origin in the yin-yang concept from Chinese alchemy, which is a joining of interdependent opposites to form a whole. It contains the beginning and ending of the story. The story starts somewhere along this side of the pentagon and proceeds clockwise to the first apex. As a matter of fact, the entire outline of the pentagon represents the time flow of conflict as indicated by the curved arrow. See the Figure 3-5.

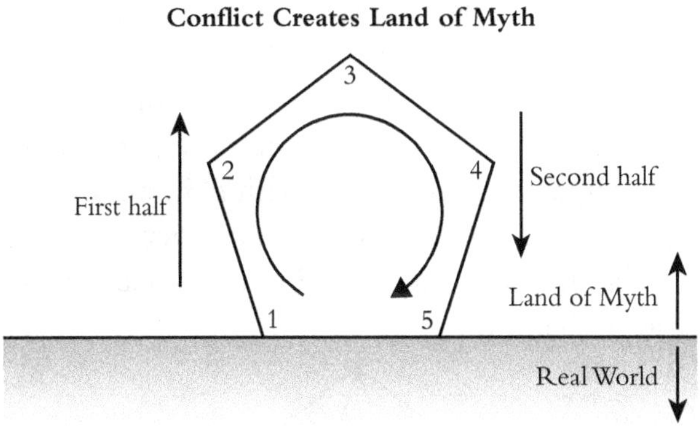

The Plot Pentagon

Conflict Creates Land of Myth

Figure 3-5 The Land of Myth

At this point let's take a second to realize that if the conflict is mediated immediately and resolved, we have no story. The yin-yang remains joined. We've missed an opportunity. All this goodwill is the death of story. It takes some hard-nose resistance and animosity to get a story going. However, if this congeniality over the conflict doesn't materialize, the yin-yang separates, and we're in business. Plot Point One, PP1, locking the conflict, lifts the story off the ground, lofts it by virtue of the emotional tension created, and sends it soaring into the Land of Story. At the apex, PP3, it reverses direction, as we said it must, and comes screaming back down toward normality where the conflict will be resolved at impact, PP5. The line connecting PP5 with PP1 contains no conflict and represents grounded normal reality.

The Land of Story, as the habitat of all myth, ancient and modern, is an ephemeral psychic space that exists in the fertile soil of the imagination. To bring your story to life in that psychic landscape, the leavening ingredient is conflict. The story contained within the pentagon exists within the Land of Myth, and we will explore that world in depth in succeeding chapters.

If we look at the pentagon just as a geometric figure, and start connecting each plot point with all the others, we see that we have constructed a five-pointed star called a pentagram. See

Figure 3-6. The ancient Greeks knew about both the pentagon and the pentagram. They knew how to construct them, and considered them to be divine objects. Pythagoras, who discovered them, adopted the pentagram as the symbol of his brotherhood, the Pythagoreans. When we constructed the pentagram, we also created another, smaller pentagon within it, although it points in the opposite direction relative to our larger one. This process of connecting dots or extending lines and faces is known in geometry as "stellation."

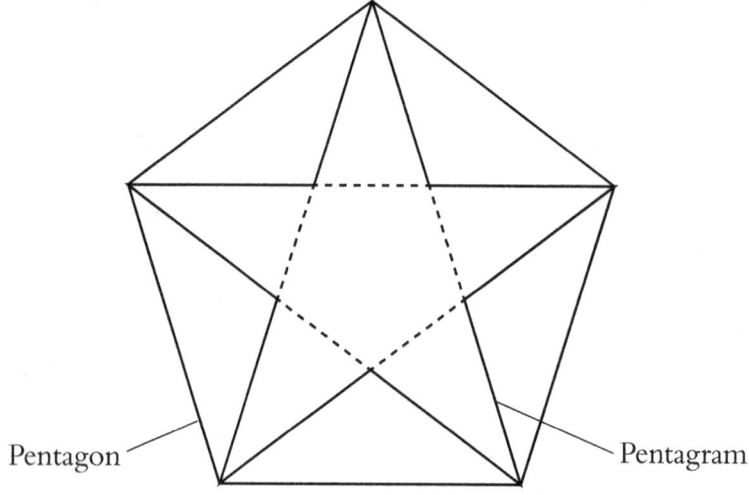

Figure 3-6 Pentagon/Pentagram

If we take this smaller pentagon as symbolic of something else going on in the story, and remembering that the pentagon represents conflict, it signifies that the external conflict between the protagonist and antagonist raises conflicts internal to each of them, something we already knew but can now symbolically visualize. Most people try to avoid conflict, apprehensive of what they may have to do to resolve it in their favor. This leads to soul-searching that the person must deal with to become fully engaged in the external conflict. The reason it's pointed in the opposite direction is that this conflict is a resisting response to the character's central plot conflict. This at least is one possible

The Plot Pentagon

interpretation of the internal pentagon.

At this point, the careful reader will notice that connecting the plot points on this internal pentagon will produce another, even smaller, pentagram and pentagon inside the original ones. Indeed, we can continue this stellation process indefinitely. However, since each pentagram/pentagon gets smaller and smaller, we might suppose that this represents uncovering different layers of personal values or psychic states and religion or spirituality. As far as an individual is concerned, we see that it has infinite depth, and if one were to accept the beliefs of many religious disciplines, somewhere inside, we'd find God.

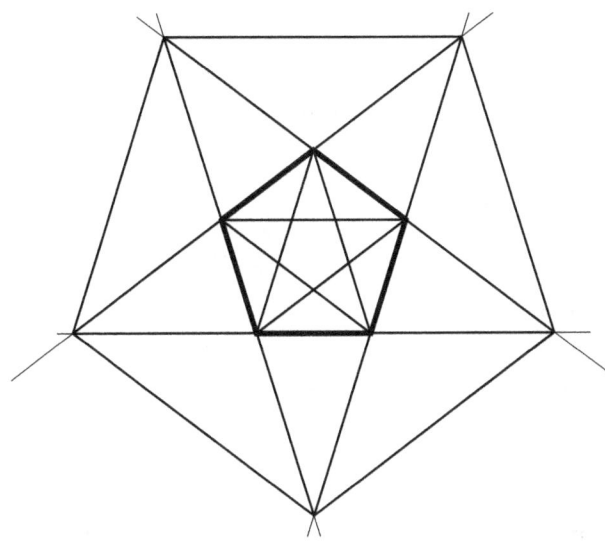

Figure 3-7 Stellation Symbol Regeneration

We can also extend the lines outside the pentagon, as in Figure 3-7, to see where that leads. At first, it creates a larger pentagram, and if we then connect its points sequentially, we have created another larger pentagon outside the plot pentagon, but again one that points in the opposite direction. What would all this external geometry mean relative to the story? This is a verification of something we already knew, i.e., that our characters may be related to a cosmic struggle. The protagonist may represent good, and the antagonist evil. In this way, we might also envision encountering God and something or someone in opposition to him out there. It would seem that somehow our story has doubled back on itself, the external becoming the equivalent of the internal, a concept you might keep in mind as we go forward.

This also represents the universal being reflected in the particular and is simply another way of saying that, within the symbol we've created, the macrocosmic meets and integrates with the microcosmic. We now know that all properly structured stories have both philosophical and psychological dimensions that give them universal as well as deeply personal significance. When properly told, all stories resonate in this way even though they don't necessarily speak openly to these other levels of meaning.

The plot diagram based on conflict is the mechanism for investigating theme and providing meaning, and at each of the five plot points, the protagonist must learn something about her/himself. The antagonist may learn something also, but our main focus, at least for now, is the protagonist.

These insights, obtained from the plot pentagon, help to fully flesh out not only our characters but the philosophical nature of the events described. The really strange, one might even say mystical, part of it is that this relationship between our plot and the pentagon doesn't feel forced. The alignment of story elements and the geometry of the pentagon isn't just coincidental. It's as if the pentagon and story structure are the same entity. Newton's Laws of Motion describe rather perfectly the dynamics of objects in the real world. The connection between mathematics (including geometry) and the natural world is a mystical one that surprised the ancient Greeks when they discovered it.

They saw numbers in nature, observing the fine structures of flowers. They saw numbers in the construction of their temples, where form followed what they considered to be the spiritual beauty of divine number relationships. They saw numbers in sculpture and art as their artists sought to represent the general makeup of shared attributes, rather than the soul of an individual. They saw numbers in their plays, built on structured themes

The Plot Pentagon

of crimes and curses. All this logic, structure, and clarity, all this love of symmetry, form, and perfection was applied to reasoning and a belief that the universe is ordered and explainable. [Mazur, page 17.]

Pythagoras played around with music and discovered the mathematical underpinning of its nature, e.g., the musical intervals of the diatonic scale. He famously said "all nature consists of harmony arising out of number." [Sir James Jeans, *Science and Music*, page 154.] Songs have had structure, or "geometry," for hundreds of years. The sonata rhondo form is one example from classical music. In popular music, the thirty-two bar form with four eight-bar sections, AABA, is frequently used. Is it any wonder then that stories also have structure? Pythagoras' statement applies to storytelling — geometry explains it all. Just as Newton discovered the elements of motion — force, location, acceleration, velocity — so we uncovered the elements of story, that its basic nature is conflict.

Another way of describing this stellation property of the pentagon is to term it "self-regenerating." As a simple geometric object in one plane, it signifies the possibility of an infinity of planes both lower and higher that starts to look a little like a wormhole. But that's not the end of its self-regenerating qualities. The fact that it was created in association with a circle and has a clockwise time flow means that it is unending — the end leads to a new beginning. This timelessness is a property of the Divine World, something we'll need to discuss further later.

The fact that conflict and theme are so indelibly linked gives rise to another pentagon — that representing the progressive unveiling of the central theme. Theme has to do with the protagonist gaining insight and awareness, an act of consciousness raising. Describing the conflict and how it progresses is a necessity, but at the same time, the author must delineate the protagonist's struggle to gradually become enlightened. This feeds directly into the author's own awakening as a part of becoming worthy. You might not quite get the connection yet, but it will become unmistakable a little later.

Of course, this isn't the first time someone proposed a five-act dramatic structure. Most notable is Dr. Gustav Freytag who did so in his *Technique of the Drama* (1900). Unfortunately, he didn't relate his structure directly to conflict, nor did he describe his five acts as a pentagon. He likened his plot structure to a pyramid. His five acts are (a) introduction, (b) rise, (c) climax [apex of the pyramid], (d) return or fall, and (e) catastrophe.

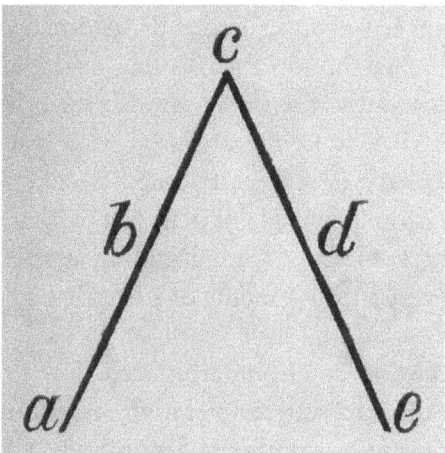

Figure 3-8 Freytag's 5 Act Structure [page 115]

He also referred to an "exciting force" that drives the action but did so without an actionable definition; however, it most certainly is conflict. All this plus his description of what goes on inside characters is the best I've read. It's a book well worth reading.

★

We have been discussing conflict as a part of imaginative storytelling, but how does story play out in real life? And the answer is that it occurs whenever we experience conflict, that is to say practically all the time. But perhaps nowhere does story become more evident in our lives than when confronted with loss, and we experience the most profound sense of loss as grief. It can be associated with the loss of a loved one, but the most intense is when we come face to face with our own death, particularly

The Plot Pentagon

if it is premature. We might even say that we experience death as an internal conflict, one between life and death. In the end, death always overcomes life. That is a really powerful premise. The situation has been studied extensively by Dr. Elizabeth Kübler-Ross. She published her findings in a book titled *On Death and Dying*. What she learned is that patients who have been told that they are terminally ill experience five stages of grief: denial, anger, bargaining, depression and acceptance. She calls them "coping mechanisms" [page 37], but I wonder if something much deeper is going on. After all, the fact that it occurs with five stages starts to sound a lot like our plot diagram, even though she's talking about what we'd term the periods between plot points. Here's how she describes a typical reaction during each phase:

Denial: *No, not me, it cannot be true.* [page 38]

Anger: ...*anger is displaced in all directions and projected into the environment at times almost at random.* [page 50]

Bargaining: *If God has decided to take us from this earth and he did not respond to my angry pleas, he may be more favorable if I ask nicely.* [page 82]

Depression: [The patient] *expressed many regrets for his "failures" when he was well, for lost opportunities while there was still time to be with his family, and sorrow at being unable to provide more for them.* [page 88]

Acceptance: *It is almost void of feelings. It is as if the pain had gone, the struggle is over, and there comes a time for "the final rest before the long journey"*... [page 113]

We could then envision an event, a plot point, triggering each phase. This is my supposition and not one made by Kübler-Ross. I would identify them as:

PP1: Notification of Impending Death — Shock (Locking the Conflict)
PP2: Confirmation of Impending Death (Conflict Escalation)
PP3: Resistance is Useless (Conflict Reversal)
PP4: Profound Realization of Coming Death (Anguish of

Choice)

PP5: Encountering Death (Conflict Resolution)

Here's how it all fits together on our plot diagram:

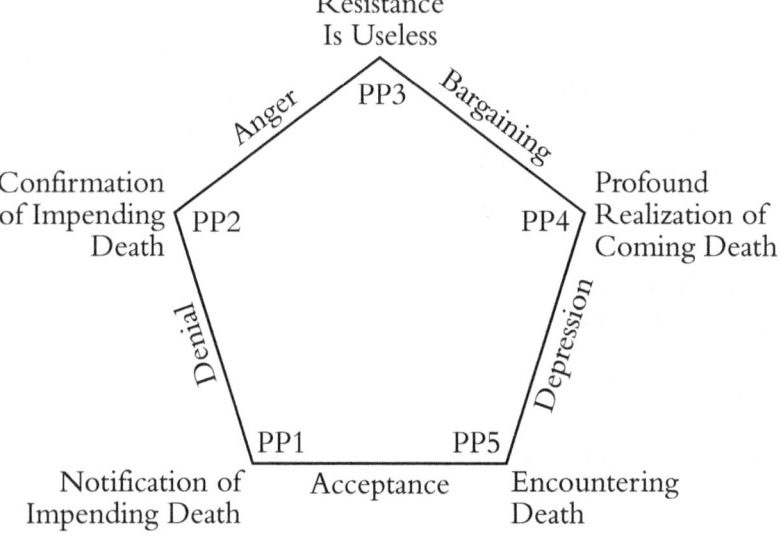

Figure 3-9 Dealing with Grief

The apparent connection between our plot diagram and Kübler-Ross's research is no coincidence. We experience life as story. We are mythical beings, and when confronted with something that seems so contradictory to our being, we have to experience it within the framework of story to fully resolve the internal conflict and emerge with a sense of meaning provided by this, the final event. Given time to accomplish this, it is the way we die. This is the way our psyche comes to terms with death. And although it may fit this five-stage pattern, each individual's experience will be unique.

We can also learn something more about the complexity of storytelling by listening to what she says about the purity of these stages. None occur as distinct, separate phases. "These [coping] means will last for different periods of time and will replace each other or exist at times side by side." [page 138] We can generate

The Plot Pentagon

a plot pentagon for our story, but in the end, we must allow the story to seek its own course through the emotional turmoil.

We might also envision the internal and external pentagons we could generate from Figure 3-9 by stellation. These larger and smaller pentagons and pentagrams would represent the internal conflicts and external issues (intellectual, psychological, moral) relative to those of external, real-world issues (spouse, family, friends, hospital, politics).

This may also play out in a normal life span. I believe what happens to solve this grief complex is that we are in a state of denial most of our lives. As we get older, we gradually see the end of our lives coming toward us, and we get mad about it, about aging. But we still have some time left, so we do things to make the most of it by entering the bargaining phase. When we become geriatric, we frequently become depressed. Many of those around us have passed on, and we can see the end of our road clearly and inevitably. But as it draws nearer, we come to accept it. Those of us who are more aware may go through this process naturally and continuously, so that in the end, it isn't such a shocking, emotionally turbulent time. It seems that when we suffer a premature death, the grieving process must occur over a much shorter time span, and it becomes more obvious. If we die in an accident, we don't get a chance to go through the grief cycle, nor do our friends and family, and that is indeed a problem because it is a normal part of the human experience. This is the struggle between life and death. Death always overcomes life.

Death is not the only event that generates the five stages of grief. Divorce, loss of a job, a financial setback, all such events can trigger the grieving process, although they will not necessarily be experienced quite so profoundly. But here's the main point. We are mythical beings, and the plot pentagon is the complete paradigm for the way we live out the conflicts of our lives.

★

Is the plot pentagon the Philosopher's Stone for storytellers? Not by a long shot. Although intriguing, it's a flat, two-dimensional object. We still have a ways to go before we come to something that profound. I've alluded to the fact that it seems to have a mystical quality, and relative to that statement, we've only begun to scratch the surface. Although not the Philosopher's Stone, I realize that discovering the plot pentagon is a big thing. Notice that I said "discovered," not created or developed. This is a discovery of something that has always existed. We found this symbol as if it were a physical object lying on the ground on which we stubbed a toe.

When we first bent the storyline "iron bar" and joined the "setup" with the "denouement," we formed a circle. To summarize a little, that circle represents the complete storyline whereupon we positioned the plot points. Plus, it's self-regenerating and has a coincident beginning and ending, and that property makes the circle look a lot like another object, the first example of which archaeologists found in an ancient Egyptian funerary text from the 14th century BC, in the tomb of Tutankhamen. Plato also mentioned this object in the *Timaeus*. It was the most basic symbol of alchemy for 1,500 years, and Carl Jung tells us that it spontaneously appears in drawings by patients undergoing psychotherapy. It is frequently an element of a mandala. This is the Ouroboros or serpent/dragon eating its own tail.

The pentagram makes something else obvious. Its five spires seemingly radiate out from the center of the circle, which is also coincident with the center of the pentagon and pentagram. This center of all activity now becomes our focus, and we shall spend some time discussing it because it'll require a little Hinduism and Buddhism to help us understand it.

I know what you're thinking: "I just came here to find out how to tell a good story. Now we've got alchemists over in the corner lighting fires, all that smoke and stink. I expected that much, but now you have ancient Greeks and Egyptians scattered about and all this talk of death and dying. You've brought Eastern religions and meditation into it. I can hear the primordial vibration of 'Omm...' in the background. Here comes Carl Jung with a horde

The Plot Pentagon

of his analytical psychologists raising a fuss. And dragons? Just where are you leading me? I'm not sure I'm ready for this."

And you're right. This is the point in *The Matrix* where Morpheus brings out the red and blue pills and asks how far down the rabbit hole you want to go. And you better not lean over too far, Alice, because you're about to fall in, and when you do, it's a scary place with no way to turn back. Once you're in, you have to fall all the way through the Earth and come out the other side.

Here, Neo, are your alternatives: Take the blue pill, and you can go back to the way you've always told stories, augmented of course by what you've already learned about plot structure. At least you'll take away something that will substantially improve your storytelling ability. Still, a ho-hum existence for an author, who could have learned so much more, but a safer state of being. Take the red pill, and you'll uncover all that's behind good storytelling, but you'll also end up learning more about yourself than you ever wanted, and possibly even more than is good for you. It will change you, and perhaps you're happy with the way you are. And it's not necessarily a safe trip either. Once you've fallen into this rabbit hole, you may need a therapist to find your way out.

I had to make that same decision. I chose the red pill and jumped off into the rabbit hole. I then spent a year learning and practicing a technique to probe the Unconscious (we'll discuss that later), following which I spent another two years delving into the far reaches of my own psyche digging up creative material for a vampire novel. But I had already spent five years in therapy with a bona fide and experienced psychiatrist. Plus, I'm older than most who will read this book, and with age comes a certain psychic stability that one doesn't necessarily have earlier in life. This is particularly true for someone going through a stressful personal situation or perhaps midlife. I know of at least three periods in my own life that seeing what I'm about to show you would not have been in my own best interest. You can take it from me that when you pull back that curtain, Dorothy, you won't see a shriveled old man turning the handle on a steam-punk engine. You'll come face-to-face with the abyss.

Remember that episode of *Buffy the Vampire Slayer* [S6:E17] where Buffy is in an asylum having suffered for many years from a schizophrenic event within which she's imagined a fictional world where she's the Chosen One and this other, psychiatric-ward world is the real one? In the hospital room, with Buffy huddled in a corner, her mother tells Buffy to have faith in herself, that she's strong enough to whip the schizophrenia and keep her mind in the real world. With this vote of confidence, Buffy says, "Thank you," and then goes back into her delusional vampire world where she is a superhero and has to regularly save the planet from a demon apocalypse.

That's what we're talking about here.

I can't guarantee you'll make it back out in one piece. This may seem overly dramatic, but where we're going is quite probably uncharted territory for you, Mr Anderson, and this is a genuine warning. The search for the Philosopher's Stone is serious business.

Red pill? Blue pill? Your choice.

CHAPTER 4 Down the Rabbit Hole

So, you've taken the red pill. Well, get ready for the ride of your life. We're after the source of your own creativity, and although it will involve investigating what seems a side issue or two, you'll have to trust that we are headed into the Land of Story. Remember that toward the end of the previous chapter, we were discussing the curious fact that the three geometric figures (pentagon, pentagram, circle) in our plot symbol are all concentric about a point from which everything seems to radiate, i.e., all the story's energy seems to originate there. This point has a name in Hinduism. It's called the "bindu" and is positioned at the center of a yantra.

In much of what follows in this chapter, we'll be discussing some aspects of Eastern religion meditation techniques. It turns out that none of these disciplines (alchemy, psychology, religion, storytelling) are that far removed from each other. Indeed, the overlap is phenomenal. Carl Jung found this to be true. Trust that the ideas we develop are in the mainstream of our quest. Without exception, they all have their origin in the human experience.

Eastern religions use yantras and mandalas as aids in meditation, which in our case would mean meditation on our story plot diagram. Yantras are geometric in nature and similar to mandalas,

Story Alchemy

which are used in Buddhism. The bindu, the dot at the center of all yantras, is what Madhu Khanna in his book titled, *Yantra, The Tantric Symbol of Cosmic Unity*, calls "the primordial seed of the universe." [page 73] He defines it as an "extensionless point, sacred symbol of the cosmos in its unmanifested state." [page 171]

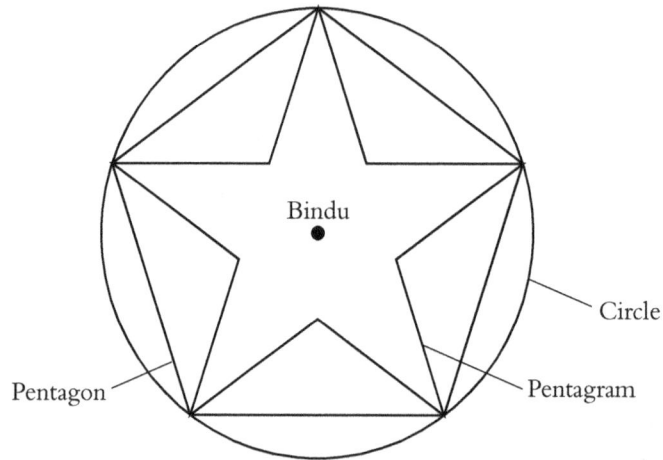

Figure 4-1 Bindu at the Center of a Yantra

This would seem to describe the center of our plot diagram perfectly because even though the self-regenerating circles, pentagons, and pentagrams are ever shrinking in size, they never touch the point in the center. They never become extensions of the bindu. The bindu is a duality and that from which all else receives its energy. That "Omm..." sound we heard toward the end of the previous chapter? Here's what Khanna has to say about it:

Particular sound-syllables are especially linked to yantras. The sound-syllable Om represents the fundamental thought-form of all-pervading reality. With its associations with the universe in all its manifestation, Om is a complete alphabetical yantra in its own right and can be equated with the creative point, the bindu. [page 37]

It seems that the bindu was calling us. This is rather remarkable because we as storytellers also have something that doesn't show

Down the Rabbit Hole

up on our plot pentagon and consists of a duality, i.e., opposing forces, and is the all-pervading reality of the fictional universe. That is the premise, which of course is the source of all things story. Now we've found where the premise has been hiding, and it is directly in the center of the circle/pentagon/pentagram, which we now realize is the bindu of a yantra.

Lest you think we've gone far afield by delving into meditation, realize that the alchemists used all these geometric figures for their own purposes. In particular, the alchemists were interested in the Vitruvian Man, especially as drawn by Leonardo da Vinci:

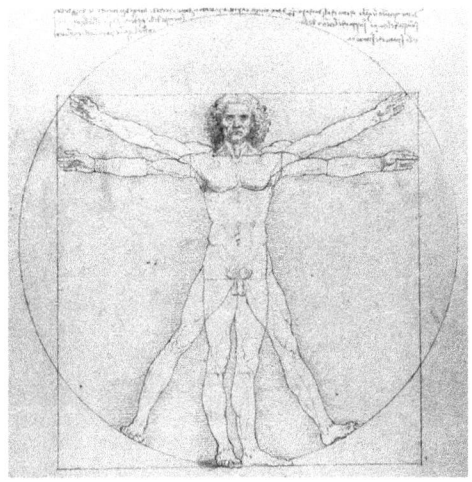

Figure 4-2 Leonardo da Vinci's Vitruvian Man

The bindu would reside at the man's navel. St. Thomas Aquinas is said to have believed that the navel is the bodily metaphor for spiritual things. Christians, and most Western alchemists were devout, allowed that the five corners represented Christ's five wounds received on the cross.

What else might the premise, being located at the geometric center and being equivalent to the bindu, tell us? The pentagram's rays interestingly meet the circle at the plot points of our pentagon. The spires of the pentagram could possibly indicate that they funnel more psychic energy from the bindu into the corners of the pentagon, the plot points, than they do to the other areas of the story so that these events have added emphasis. These are the critical events in the story that must be dramatized and not told in narrative summary.

Back in Chapter 2 when we developed our premise, the prima materia, we realized that our entire story derived from it by virtue of it identifying the central conflict. The energy from the premise drives the entire story. Now we learn that, not only is it the center of the plot diagram, but it also explains the origin of the five plot points and what causes the pronounced effect they have on the story. This is the pentagram's funneling effect on bindu radiation.

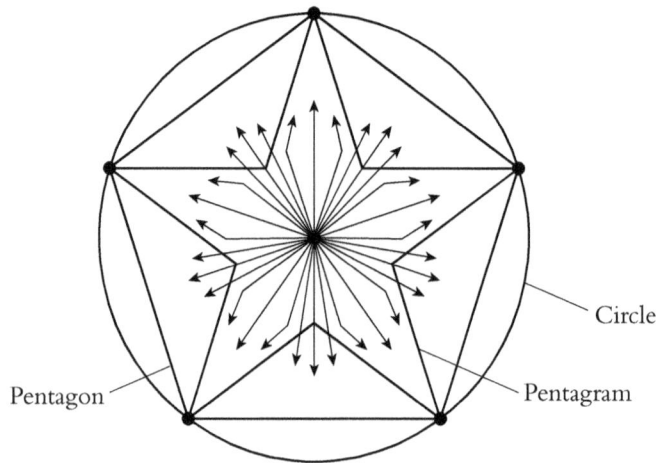

Figure 4-3 Bindu Radiation

Let's state it all once again. The pentagram and the pentagon are partners in the plotting process. The pentagram is, seemingly, the creator of the plot points. This effect, in the form of psychic energy, comes directly from the bindu, the premise, which drives the story. All points along a circle are equal creating the gradual curve, but all points along the story pentagon are not weighted equally, and the five corner points along it specifically denote a change in line direction. This is the quantization of story. While time's arrow circumnavigates the story, the bindu (premise) is pulsing, radiating psychic energy to the entire storyline but providing the most energy to the five plot points through

Down the Rabbit Hole

pentagram funneling.

I would remind you that our plot yantra/mandala is a symbol, and as such, nothing on it contains information specific to your story, not even the premise, because the geometry is also a generic concept. It is just a statement of opposing wills and contains the nature of the conflict and its resolution. Yet every item in it tells you something you need to know about plotting your story. Your idea must be draped over this structure. You have to find the elements of your story that correspond to the milestones indicated in the plot diagram. It's all very much the underlying mathematics of storytelling, as Pythagoras would have envisioned.

But the plot pentagon is more than just a static symbol. It's a dynamic, pulsing machine that comes to life during storytelling. The planets orbit the Sun without ever touching it, yet life on Earth depends on the energy of sunlight. In the same way, the bindu provides both the energy to power the story and the light (enlightenment) that provides meaning. The pentagram spires are like detached flames that lick the five primary plot points. The bindu is also the axis about which the story pivots. How many times have you read the synopsis of a movie and it started out with the statement that "The story revolves around..."? That characterization doesn't happen by accident. As shown in Figure 4-4, the bindu pulses, and the plot points flash in sequence. It's a cosmic symbol that comes to life through character.

Yes, I realize we have forgotten alchemy's tail-eating, fire-breathing dragon, and we will spend more time with it, but not just yet. Hang on for just a little longer.

When we bent that iron bar into a circle and created the plot pentagon, it seemed such a benign act. Instead, what we've done may be likened more accurately to creating a wormhole. I'm not talking about something that a nightcrawler might wiggle its way through into the earth, and not Alice's rabbit hole either, although that is a rather interesting analogy. I'm talking about the wormhole that is an outgrowth of Einstein's General Relativity, the cosmological Einstein-Rosen Bridge, which is a shortcut through the space-time continuum. Okay, that might be a bit of an overstatement, but not by much as you'll see when I introduce you to the Iris of Time in a later chapter.

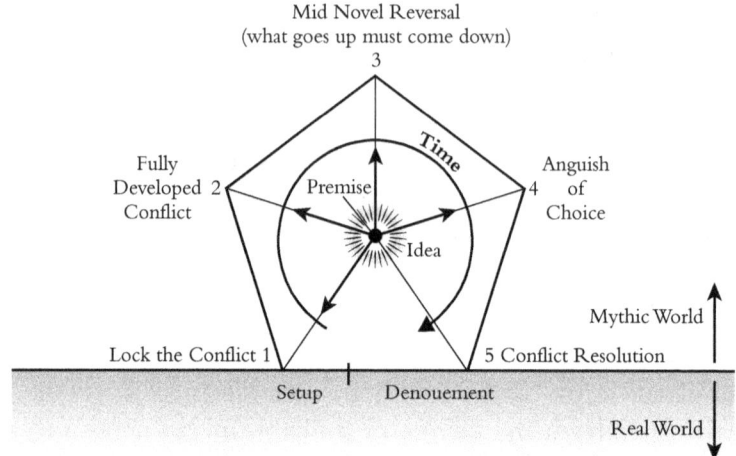

Figure 4-4 Fully Functional Plot Diagram

So how does it work? I mean really, what's going on here?

Yantras are geometric machines that funnel resonant energy from the Cosmos into the psyche, somewhat like a crystal radio or the sympathetic acoustical resonance of the wind and the strings of an Aeolian harp. Yantras also serve as revelatory channels for cosmic truth. Here's how Madhu Khanna describes the yantra:

Despite its cosmic meanings a yantra is a reality lived. Because of the relationship that exists in the Tantras [Hindu or Buddhist religious ritual texts] *between the outer world (the macrocosm) and man's inner world (the microcosm), every symbol in the yantra is ambivalently resonant in inner-outer synthesis, and is associated with the subtle body and aspects of human consciousness. Thus, for instance, the bindu in a yantra is cosmic when viewed as the emblem of the Absolute Principle but psychological when it is related to the adept's spiritual centre. By aligning these two planes of awareness, the yantra translates psychic realities into cosmic terms and the cosmos into psychic planes.* [page 21/2]

It would seem that from "a reality lived" we could infer the

Down the Rabbit Hole

psychic reality of a well-told story. All this business about inner and outer worlds parallels what we've said about the replicating pentagons and pentagrams through stellation. It seems that since we constructed our yantra using proven storytelling principles, it will be well suited for meditation on stories because it will resonate with the psychic energy of which Khanna speaks.

Before we get into how to meditate on this yantra, I want to talk a bit about the dynamics of storytelling. And I have another confession, well two actually. On May 19, 2010, I started practicing a technique for probing the unconscious, but specifically modified as a procedure for authors to use during the creative process. I focused on this activity for one year, and then I started using what I learned to write a vampire novel. Just weeks before I started writing that novel, on March 9, 2011, I had a dream of a dragon. Here's what I wrote about the dream the next morning:

Sometime during the night, I had a dream of a wild animal loose upon the land. I don't know where I was, but I was with a bunch of people, families with children, and we heard that a huge animal was on its way toward us, something wild and deadly.

We all left our homes and ran to hide among some large objects stacked in a row at the edge of a field. The square objects were huge, something similar to haystacks, although the bails were much larger. They had spaces between them that we could squeeze between. It was night, but we could see a little, as if a full moon was out.

The huge objects didn't slow the animal at all. It ran on all fours and was long and scaly, shaped like an alligator, the size of a tank, only much longer. It used its snout to scatter the stacks we were hidden among. To escape, we ran across the plowed field to the far side among the deserted buildings of a small town, a hamlet.

The animal destroyed the row of stacked objects all the way to the end of the field, apparently not seeing us as we ran from him. He then turned along the far side of the field, destroyed homes in the far corner of the field and then turned back toward us and the deserted homes, among which we were now hiding. We could hear him coming. We ran among the buildings as he got closer, each man and child for himself. The animal was breathing fire, and although I didn't realize it in my dream, it was a dragon, a non-flying dragon, much like a huge Komodo dragon the size of a train engine. I ran down a deserted street between closely spaced buildings. The dragon saw me and came after me. I ran around the back of a building with him in hot pursuit, blowing flames and consuming everything in his path. I tried to double back and come up behind him, but when I turned the corner, there he was directly in front of me, only a few paces away. I had no chance of escape. One breath and I'd be fried.

But the dragon didn't breathe fire on me. He stopped and stared at me. I stood in front of him, not moving, ready to accept my fate. But the dragon didn't seem hostile. He came towards me, stopped, and then shoved something in front of me. He was giving me something. It was a loosely packed block of a compressed straw-like substance, dark gray-green, that I recognized. It was a rare food substance highly sought after. It was an offering of friendship. I took it into my hands, and looked up to talk to the dragon, but then my dream ended.

Time and again, I revisited what I'd written about the dream, but it never seemed to mean anything, never quite made sense. Two years later, two things about the dream stood out. First, if you remember, we have a dragon circling our plot pentagon, our storytelling mandala. My dream dragon circled the community where I was living, a seemingly meaningless if not bizarre action then, but one that later made sense within a mandala context. It was as if my dream occurred within the storytelling mandala, and that my dream community also was there.

Second, I received a gift from the dragon, seemingly a peace offering. I didn't realize it at the time, but I now believe that the gift had to do with a story I had been contemplating. Actually, I believe that this dream came two weeks before I thought of writing a vampire novel. I had yet to decided on a subject. I believe that the gift, that dark gray-green substance from my dragon, somehow empowered that process. The gift was a food substance that provided the psychic energy to facilitate the creative process. Therefore, I associated the dragon of my dream with this dragon, the Ouroboros, and the gift with my vampire story.

Down the Rabbit Hole

Here's what David Fontana says about dragons associated with mandalas:

The dragon is the paradox of being — light and dark, creation and destruction, male and female, and the unifying force of these opposites. The dragon's fire is the primal energy of the physical world. [*Meditating with Mandalas*, page 141]

Aristotle tells us that the story should be one continuous action. The circle, the Ouroboros, represents that action as it completes one cycle. It seems that the dragon made one circle of our community before confronting me and then providing a gift, the primal energy necessary to activate my vampire story. That gift would power the premise, the bindu, at the center.

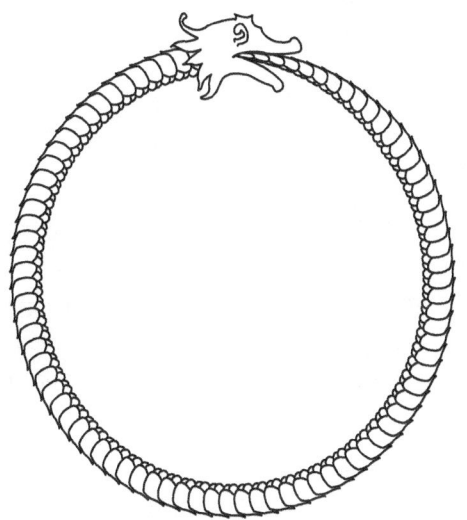

Figure 4-5 Ouroboros

It's instructive to make a clear distinction between a yantra and a mandala, at least in the manner we'll be referring to them. The yantra we'll view as a purely geometric symbol, and we'll identify it with the bindu, pentagon, pentagram, and circle. Our use of the mandala will be more life oriented, and we'll associate it with the dragon in place of the circle, and the five Buddhas of enlightenment (I'll define these in Chapter 7) instead of the plot points of the pentagon.

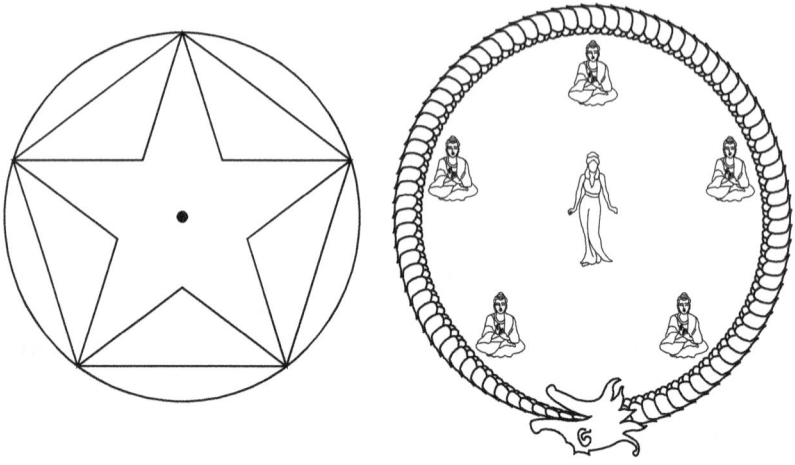

Figure 4-6 Yantra — Mandala

How would we go about meditating on such a yantra/mandala to generate material for a particular story? David Fontana describes the process this way:

Many successful visual artists... are open to a creative impulse that arises from deep levels of the unconscious. The artist expresses what is given to him or her, not what is put together by conscious thought. ...the modern creative artist has to allow some inner impulse to take over from his own mind and express itself through the person, rather than from the person. [page 25]

Carl Jung has taken this a step further for us by developing a method, which puts the individual's Consciousness right up against the Unconscious, from where all this channeled psychic energy originates. We will combine his psychological principles with Eastern religion, interpret each to suit the storyteller, and develop a procedure to accomplish the task at hand.

But we still have a couple of things to take care of first. Before using his meditation technique, you need to know more of Jung's theory of the Unconscious.

CHAPTER 5 The Dark Realm of the Unconscious

What is the Unconscious? It is the mind's processes, which are not available for introspection. Said another way, we are not aware of these mental processes. They go on, so to speak, without us. We normally do not realize the presence or understand the influence of the Unconscious on our thoughts. It appears spontaneously in dreams as a dark lake with lots of frightening creatures lurking within. Jung divided the Unconscious into two components: the Personal and the Collective. Here's what he says of the Personal Unconscious, which he calls the Shadow:

[The Shadow] *owes its existence to the simple fact that all the impulses, thoughts, wishes, and tendencies which run counter to the rational orientation of daily life are denied expression, thrust into the background, and finally fall into the unconscious. There all the things which we have repressed and suppressed, which we have deliberately ignored and devalued, gradually accumulate and, in time, acquire such force that they begin to influence consciousness.* [*Civilization in Transition*, "The Role of the Unconscious," para 25]

We created our own Shadow while we were young during socialization when we had to suppress a lot of our natural tendencies, but it's also been added to almost continuously since.

It's not difficult to see that this is a place of conflict, resentment, trouble beyond imagining, and therefore, a marvelous place for the author to pursue story material. The problem of course is that, once unleashed, the Shadow can wreak havoc in Consciousness, at least under certain conditions. We do have safeguards, such as they are, against getting flooded by this Shadow material, and we'll get to them a little later.

But the Shadow isn't the larger or even the most interesting part of the Unconscious. That larger part is called the Collective Unconscious, which Jung defines as follows:

[The Shadow] *rests upon a deeper layer, which does not derive from personal experience and is not a personal acquisition but is inborn. This deeper layer I call the collective unconscious. I have chosen the term "collective" because this part of the unconscious is not individual but universal; in contrast to the personal psyche, it has contents and modes of behaviour that are more or less the same everywhere and in all individuals. It is, in other words, identical in all men and thus constitutes a common psychic substrate of a suprapersonal nature which is present in every one of us.*

…The contents of the personal unconscious are chiefly the feeling-toned complexes, as they are called; they constitute the personal and private side of psychic life. The contents of the collective unconscious, on the other hand, are known as archetypes. [*Archetypes of the Collective Unconscious*, pages 3-4, para 3-4]

If the Shadow is a dark lake, the Collective Unconscious is a vast ocean teeming with beings beyond imagining. Or actually, it is quite within our imaginative grasp if we have the courage to develop the tools necessary to navigate and mine this Universe of Unbelievability.

These two aspects of the Unconscious are not universally identified. Freud only recognized the Personal Unconscious and practiced what is known as regression therapy, i.e., retrieving and resolving childhood trauma. Freudian psychology is therefore principally about the Shadow, although he didn't call it that.

The Dark Realm of the Unconscious

His therapeutic process is certainly worthwhile, but what we're after is the whole enchilada, and Jung is the only one who can lead us into the even darker and more mysterious world of the Collective Unconscious. Freud's work is primarily of interest in the medical field, but Jung's work, although equally effective for emotionally disturbed patients, is also aligned with the creative side of humanity. It's not solely intended for use in psychotherapy and is associated with the arts.

Here comes the problem. To get a clear view of the Collective Unconscious, we first must deal with the Personal Unconscious, the Shadow. The Shadow was generated during our formative years but always involved elements of the Collective Unconscious. As stated before, the contents of the Shadow are the repressed and suppressed elements of our psyche that were not socially acceptable. That's why an author's first work is frequently a coming-of-age novel.

I have another confession. Back in 1986, after years of trying to write a novel with limited success, I took a course in creative writing at the University of Colorado from the poet Renate Wood (1938-2007). One of the first exercises she gave the class was to write a short piece of fiction about a character who was as different from ourselves as we could imagine. I immediately had an idea about a kid who was a senior in high school, belligerent, and fighting a lot. Although I'd been writing seriously for fifteen years, mostly poetry (I'd given up on novels), this was the hottest story I'd ever put on paper. Dr Wood liked what I wrote, and it was the first time I'd been told that I was writing publishable work. Three years later I had finished the rough draft of what was to become my first and bestselling novel, *The Escape of Bobby Ray Hammer*, and it came directly from that class assignment.

Dr Wood had pulled a dirty trick on everyone in the class. She had introduced each of us to our own Shadow. Dr Wood was very much into Jungian psychology, so she certainly knew what she was doing. I kept in touch with Ms Wood, and she would later suggest I might consider seeing a therapist because I seemed

Story Alchemy

to be struggling emotionally. Actually, I was already in therapy. Here's the problem expressed in a letter from CG Jung to Alice Raphael on June 7, 1955:

> The risk is, that the artifex [in our case the author] becomes identical with the goal of his opus. He becomes inflated and crazy: "multi perierunt in opere nostro!" [many have perished in our work!] There is a "demon" in the prima materia, that drives people crazy. [PhilemonFoundation.org]

The statement "many have perished in our work!" is an alchemical saying often quoted by Jung [*Jung on Alchemy*, page 2]. Since it comes from the alchemists, a certain amount of histrionics is undoubtedly involved, but it does allude to a real danger for some. I didn't realize until years later that my writing had driven me into therapy. Six months into it, I started having panic attacks. After five years, I came out the other side, having gone, as it were, through the center of the cyclone. Not only that, it wreaked havoc on my personal and professional life. Writing can also do that because of its therapeutic aspects. If you're getting to the good stuff, it can have its way with you. What had driven me into therapy had come from my Shadow, much of it from an almost fatal encounter with my father when I was twenty. Five years after starting writing that novel, which also involved father-son conflict, I was so emotionally and intellectually invested in writing that I quit my day job, and I've never gone back to astronautical engineering. So see? Writing with the intensity that I'm going to make available to you can have life-altering implications.

When we write something as long as a novel or screenplay, we deal with material from more than just the Shadow. The Collective Unconscious always plays a role. This is the reason it is possible for you to write a good, well-plotted novel or screenplay without knowing about the plot pentagon. When we have a direct line to the Unconscious, stories can intuitively come out that way. Particularly if you've been writing since you were five. For those of us who have not, it takes more conscious

The Dark Realm of the Unconscious

knowledge of the process, and that comes with the plot pentagon and dodecahedron. For you, I've gone a step beyond what Dr Wood did for me. I've hardwired you to both your Shadow and Collective Unconscious.

The good news is that both the Shadow and the Collective Unconscious contain material that is great for storytelling. The elements of the Shadow are certainly recognizable, but much of the contents of the Collective Unconscious may be rather foreign.

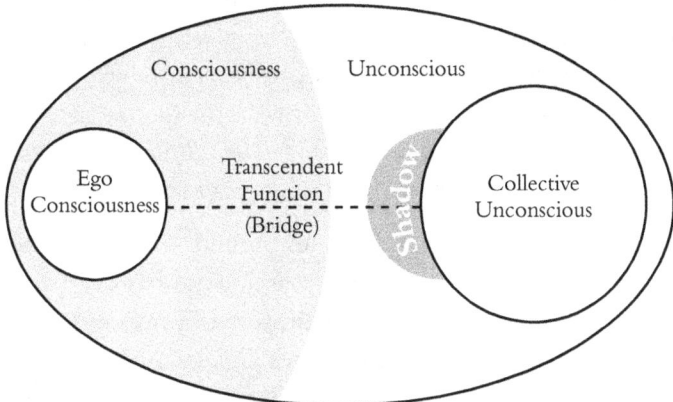

Figure 5-1 Psychic Space

How does this material from the Collective Unconscious appear to us when we experience it? Although material from the Shadow is psychologically "hot" and burns its way into a story, the elements of the Collective Unconscious when we encounter them in storytelling can be even more profoundly energized. The interesting thing is that they come in the form of primordial images, archetypes. Here's what Jung has to say:

The primordial image, or archetype, is a figure... that constantly recurs in the course of history... therefore, it is a mythological figure... When we examine these images more closely, we find that they give form to countless typical experiences of our ancestors. They are, so to speak, the psychic residua of innumerable experiences of the same type. They present a picture of psychic life in the average, divided up and projected into the manifold figures of the mythological pantheon. ... In each of these images there is a little piece of human psychology and human fate, a remnant of the joys and sorrows that have been repeated countless times in our ancestral history, and on the average follow ever the same course. It is like a deeply graven river-bed in the psyche, in which the waters of life, instead of flowing along as before in a broad but shallow stream, suddenly swell into a mighty river. This happens whenever that particular set of circumstances is encountered which over long periods of time has helped to lay down the primordial image.

The moment when this mythological situation reappears is always characterized by a peculiar emotional intensity; it is as though chords in us were struck that had never resounded before, or as though forces whose existence we never suspected were unloosed… At such moments we are no longer individuals, but the race; the voice of all mankind resounds in us. [*The Spirit in Man, Art, and Literature*, pages 81/2]

It seems that this phenomenon should have been noticed before. Do we have any evidence that anyone has ever stumbled into it while writing fiction? The answer is a resounding, "Yes!" It happens all the time, but rarely does an author write about the experience. When they do, it can be an eye-opening lesson for all of us. Consider the case of Mary Shelley and how she came upon the idea for her first novel, *Frankenstein*. In the summer of 1816, Mary, nineteen at the time, went to bed one evening after a late night discussion with Percy Shelley and Lord Byron concerning the reanimation of dead matter and the nature of life. She had been for some time trying to come up with an idea for a ghost story without success. What happened that night when she tried to sleep, she describes in her own words for the 1831 edition of *Frankenstein*:

When I placed my head on the pillow, I did not sleep, nor could I be said to think. My imagination, unbidden, possessed and guided me, gifting the successive images that arose in my mind with a vividness far beyond the usual bounds of reverie. I saw—with shut eyes, but acute mental vision—I saw the pale student of unhallowed arts kneeling beside the thing he had put together. I saw the hideous phantasm of a man

The Dark Realm of the Unconscious

stretched out, and then, on the working of some powerful engine, show signs of life, and stir with an uneasy, half-vital motion. Frightful must it be; for supremely frightful would be the effect of any human endeavour to mock the stupendous mechanism of the Creator of the world. ...he might sleep in the belief that the silence of the grave would quench forever the transient existence of the hideous corpse which he had looked upon as the cradle of life. He sleeps; but he is awakened; he opens his eyes; behold, the horrid thing stands at his bedside, opening his curtains and looking on him with yellow, watery, but speculative eyes.

I opened mine in terror. The idea so possessed my mind, that a thrill of fear ran through me... I recurred to my ghost story—my tiresome, unlucky ghost story! O! if I could only contrive one which would frighten my reader as I myself had been frightened that night!

In concentrating on her ghost story at such a late hour just before sleep when her mind was already prepared — one might say over-prepared — for a psychic encounter, she was in direct contact with the Collective Unconscious. She saw images. They animated. She noticed the immediate hostility, conflict, inherent in her vision. She was emotionally engaged to the point of being terrorized by the vision. This was her prima materia. In using this psychic content for her novel, she "created" two of the most powerful archetypes of human existence: the mad scientist and his monstrous creation.

Those two archetypes would fascinate her 19th century world and that of the 20th and 21st centuries as well. And tell her story, she did. The story Mary fashioned in the coming months caught the public's attention immediately after publication, and through some 200 years, has never gone out of print. Indeed, the story is much alive today, hardly a year going by without another variation of it appearing on the big screen. The scientific discoveries of nuclear energy and DNA engineering have caused a lot of concern about the direction life on Earth has taken. We're concerned that our use of scientific discoveries might destroy us, and we frequently use Mary's story as a metaphor to illustrate the magnitude of the problem.

Story Alchemy

Since story is about conflict, I need to address the types of conflict that come from the Shadow and the Collective Unconscious and what characterizes each. I don't want to go too far in stereotyping the two, but they are most certainly different. The types of conflict that come from the Shadow, for normal people with rather benign childhoods, tend to be shallow personal stuff. They result in bickering and pettiness and in the end aren't always that interesting. And this is where Richard Walter's comment concerning enlightened, reasonable, rational discourse and courtesy, consideration, and consensus being boring runs into trouble. Nothing is more boring than trivial, unmotivated, trumped-up conflict. We've all tried to sit through movies that concern only the bickering of sibling rivalries and/or pointless power struggles.

Remember that the Shadow is about the conflicts we suffered and lost when becoming socialized, so you know it's not always going to be profound. But family issues and power struggles arise from the Collective Unconscious as well as the Shadow, so it's not a total loss by any means. It's just that if your story stays with material from the Shadow, it'll never be as profound as one that also pulls from the Collective Unconscious, and may never get far beyond the trivialities of life.

The conflicts that come from the Collective Unconscious are grander in scope, and although they still may be about power, the themes are more cosmic. This is where death, war and religious themes reside. Great love stories like *Romeo and Juliette* have their origin there. Vampire stories also, unicorns and centaurs. They are about death and resurrection, mortality, suffering, spirituality, Heaven and Hell. Just so you understand that it's not only adult material that comes from there, this is the Land of the Fairytale. Here's a quote from Marie Louise van Franz's *Interpretation of Fairy Tales*:

> Fairy tales are the purest and simplest expression of collective unconscious psychic processes. Therefore their value for the scientific investigation of the unconscious exceeds that of all other material. They

The Dark Realm of the Unconscious

represent the archetypes in their simplest, barest and most concise form. [page 1]

Classics such as *Cinderella, Alice and Wonderland, Rapunzel, Hansel and Gretel, Sleeping Beauty,* all are told at least partially from the Collective Unconscious. But don't get the idea that this is a static place. The archetypes evolve, as do all aspects of human existence. They manage to express their dynamic positions from within the depths of the psyche. And yes, the Collective Unconscious heavily influences stories like *The Matrix*, which has central themes about enslavement and false realities.

As stated before, the Shadow and the Collective Unconscious are not fully disconnected and unrelated. In the way I've graphically drawn them above in Figure 5-1, I've shown the two joined. The truth is traumas that create the Shadow can activate a resonate portion of the Collective Unconscious. This can create a profound psychological disturbance that rocks an individual's psychic space. No one gets out of this life without being tried.

Now that we understand our relationship with the Collective Unconscious, we can more fully come to terms with what constitutes meaning within a story, a subject we left somewhat ambiguous in Chapter 2. Meaning results from a process of increasing degrees of abstraction — from characters engaged in conflict, to the nature of that conflict, to theme, and from theme to meaning. At the end of the abstraction, theme must match up to and resonate with something within the Collective Unconscious for meaning to become apparent. Just as archetypes exist within the Collective Unconscious, so do the elements that provide meaning, divine truths, and they exist within all of us. They correspond to what Plato described as "forms" that exist in the Divine World. (See *Parmenides* Paras 129-134.) They provide wisdom. Plato saw our world as simply a metaphor of the Divine World, and for something to be meaningful in our world, it must bear a significant relationship to its counterpart within the Divine World. Meaning occurs when theme meets up with a priori knowledge in the Collective Unconscious. When that match takes place, we get a spark of psychic light that we interpret as enlightenment. Graphically, this process looks like this:

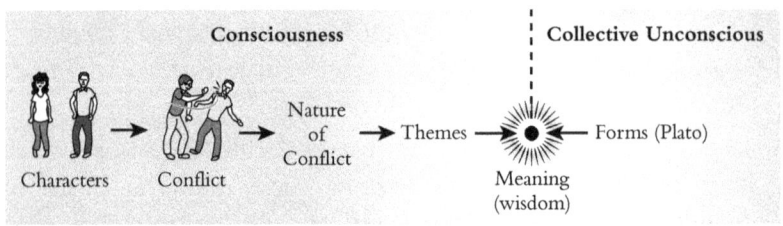

Figure 5-2 Degrees of Abstraction

Meaning in its purest sense is confirmation from the Collective Unconscious. Just as the creative impulse spontaneously generates from the Collective Unconscious, meaning also seemingly comes out of nowhere but ultimately is traceable to an impulse from the Collective Unconscious. We speak of truth as something that just makes sense, but that's because it resonates with a region of the psyche where such processes are not available for introspection.

★

We now have some of the tools to help us locate our story material and even a way of organizing it, a good portion of it anyway. What we're after is a process to mine the treasure trove of the Collective Unconscious. We have a plot pentagon in the form of a yantra/mandala, and we know that both yantras and mandalas are used as aids during meditation. Is this the full story? Do we have all the ingredients? Of course, the answer is no. What about sub-plots and narration? Story structure is much more complex. Where are the missing elements?

Let's take another stab at that Philosopher's Stone.

CHAPTER 6 The Philosopher's Stone

Stories are complex, and so far we've only addressed the premise and plot. We've made no mention of a narrator, the one who tells the story. For novels and particularly playwrights and screenwriters, the author might say, "That's me. I tell the story." But that's not true. The author always creates the narrator, consciously or unconsciously. We speak of this as the author finding his/her "voice." But most authors write in many narrative voices. For a novel, the narrator is easy to identify, but more difficult for the theatre and the big and small screen. Sometimes they do have a voiceover, but the "narrator" or storytelling element is a combination of writing, directing, photography, and scene editing. It still has a style, and that is effectively a narration because it constitutes the way the collaborators choose to tell the story — its point of view. In any case, the narrator is an element in the story, and it has no place as yet on our plot pentagon/mandala.

Subplots are also missing from our depiction of storytelling. Not only do stories have a central plot, but also several subplots, which broaden the subject matter and help the story to spread out and occupy the entire fictional world. Subplots are sub-conflicts that have all the components of the central conflict, including a premise for each. All these sub-conflicts have to be locked and resolved, just as does the central conflict. And yes, they have all five plot points. The author should identify the characters involved in these sub-conflicts and draw a plot pentagon/mandala for each. And yes, each sub-conflict has an associated theme.

Once that's accomplished, one might well wonder how all these plot pentagons relate to each other. They certainly have a relationship in the story, so we might also ask if a geometric metaphor exists that illustrates this connection. Any such diagram would of necessity be quite complex.

Where to start?

If we connect a sub-plot pentagon to each of the five sides of the main conflict pentagon, we get this:

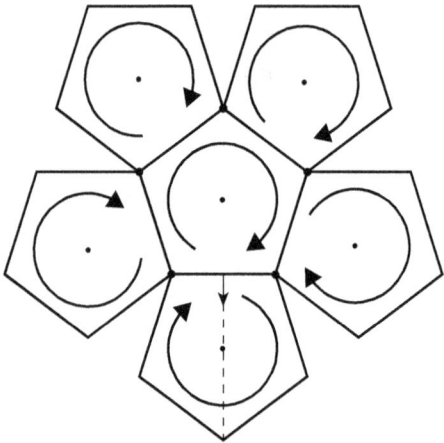

Figure 6-1 Plot/Sub-Plot Pentagon

The pentagons are connected and apparently somewhat sequenced. As each accomplishes a circular motion in time, its story unfolds. The plot pentagons are connected but not dependent on each other. This is the same as in real life. We all lead separate lives, and each of us is the hero of our own story. We tell the story from a primary point of view, generally but not necessarily, that of the protagonist. I have constructed what I call a sub-plot pentagon (see Figure 6-2) for the protagonist of the Civil War story I mentioned in Chapter 2 and provided a series of possible conflicts and sub-conflicts associated with it.

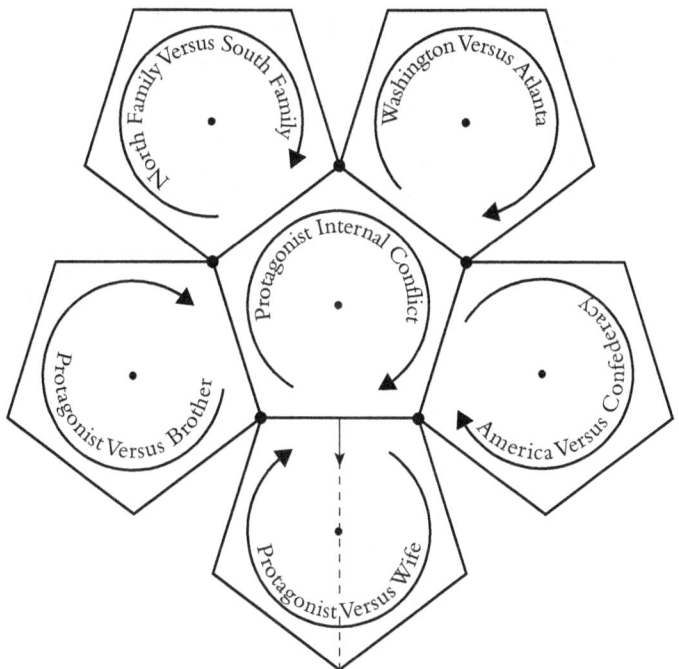

Figure 6-2 Protagonist Sub-Plot Diagram

My experience has been that to fully flesh out any character, the author has to write the character from their particular point of view. This would mean that each character should get some time in the drivers seat, so to speak, and their interaction with other characters told from their own point of view. The author has to spend a certain amount of time inside the head of each of his/her characters. This material should then be integrated into the story as told from the story's point-of-view character.

I would also take this lack of dependence as a sign that chaos plays a role in storytelling. We've imposed some pretty strict rules on plotting, but over-plotting leads to a contrived storyline. Therefore, once you achieve a modest level of plotting, let chaos play its role. It has to have a role because life is to a certain extent chaotic. Not all songs have the same thirty-two bar form either.

If we print out this connected set of five pentagons on construction paper and cut out the figure, we can then bend down the exposed pentagons, creasing the common edge with the central plot pentagon, until the edges of all five external pentagons touch. This creates a three-dimensional object that represents a good number of our sub-plots. See Figure 6-3.

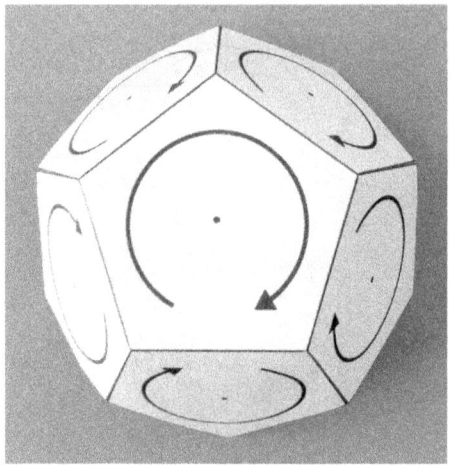

Figure 6-3 Paper Cutout Plot/Sub-Plot Pentagon

If we print out another of these sets of pentagons, cut and fold as we did the first set, and then turn it over, we have a pair of bowl-shaped pentagons:

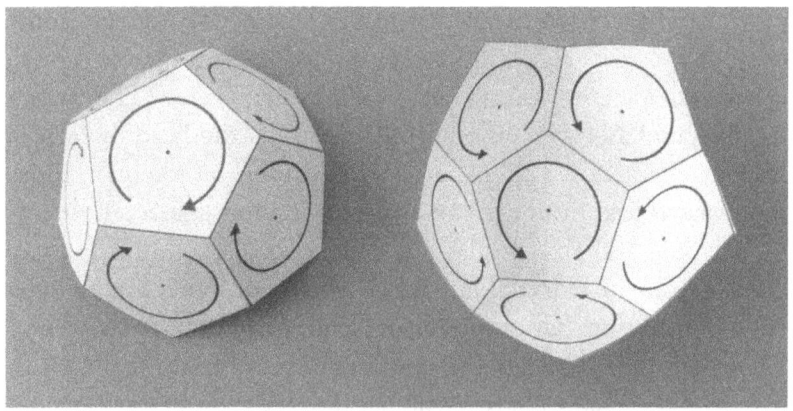

Figure 6-4 Two Bowl-Shaped Pentagons

Notice that the arrow indicating story progression in this second set, viewed from the inside now, goes counterclockwise instead of clockwise, something I'll come back to in a minute. The crazy thing about these two bowl-shaped halves is that the irregular edges look as if they'll fit together. When we try to mate these two halves, we rotate the second one 180 degrees, and then they slip up against each other and fit perfectly. They form a twelve-sided three-dimensional object called a dodecahedron.

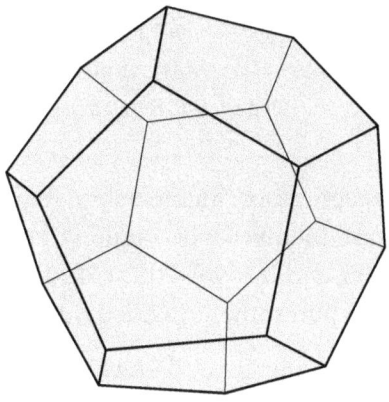

Figure 6-5 Dodecahedron - 12 Interconnected Pentagons

Now you get the euphoric feeling that we have come up against something truly distinctive. The ancient Greeks, and yes again it was the Pythagoreans, also knew about the dodecahedron. It is one of what we now know as the Platonic Solids. The dodecahedron had a special meaning for the Pythagorean Brotherhood. They saw each pentagon as representing a constellation, and since they recognized twelve, they reasoned that the dodecahedron represented the Zodiac. The Pythagoreans viewed the dodecahedron as a divine model used by the gods to create the Universe. [Plato, *The Timaeus*, 55] And get this, the constellations were the heavenly representations of many of the heroes of mythological fame. They associated a myth with each segment of this geometric object — a perfect storytelling device. The Pythagoreans saw the dodecahedron as a divine geometric symbol, and they kept it secret. Only the worthy could know of its existence.

★

As an aside, and to illustrate just how serious this worthiness issue was to the ancients, the Pythagoreans wouldn't let just anyone into their brotherhood. A prolonged probationary period followed admission:

[Pythagoras] *subjected* [the new member] *to contempt for three years, to test how he was disposed to stability and true love of learning, and if he was sufficiently equipped against popular repute so as to despise honor. After this, he ordered a five year silence for those coming to him, testing how they were disposed to self-control, since more difficult than other forms of self-control is mastery of the tongue...* [Riedweg, *Pythagoras*, page 101]

Despite these egregious membership requirements, we do have a record of one follower who couldn't keep his mouth shut about secret matters, and it involved the dodecahedron. This also illustrates the severe punishment handed out in such cases:

The Pythagorean Hippasus of Metapontum is supposed to have been the first to betray the secret by drawing the sphere consisting of twelve congruent pentagons (the pentagonal dodecahedron must have been — like the pentagram — an important Pythagorean secret symbol), whereupon he drowned in the sea as a godless blasphemer. [Riedweg, *Pythagoras*, page 26]

Note the mention of not just pentagons and the dodecahedron, but also a sphere containing them, possibly the biggest secret of all. I'll get to this a little later. The fact that we know such secrets today is in no small part because of leaks in this select society. They changed the direction of Western Civilization. Word of such forbidden knowledge spread quickly in the ancient world, and Greece benefited greatly when these discoveries became common knowledge.

★

The Pythagoreans associated the five corners of the pentagon with the four elements, earth, water, air, fire, and added a fifth, spirit. At first glance, this seems simply naive reasoning from the ancient world. After all, we have 118 elements in the Periodic Table. But

The Philosopher's Stone

it isn't as simplistic as you might think. We could associate this ancient categorization system with, not the elements, but our five states of matter: solids, liquids, gases, plasmas, and we could also add a psychic or spiritual element. Seemingly, this represents Earth and its inhabitants. The number twelve also plays an important role in ancient Greek religion. The Olympian gods, who ruled over Earth and Heaven, were twelve in number. In our modern world, Christians are well versed in Christ's Twelve Apostles. Each apex of a dodecahedron joins the corners of three pentagons so that the Trinity might also play a part.

It would be easy to lapse into thinking that this model of the cosmos is something that should be relegated to the ancient world; however, some of our most brilliant cosmologists today are proposing a model for the Universe known as the Poincaré Dodecahedral Space, which seemingly explains more cosmological data than other theories. This relates back favorably to the Pythagoreans and their belief that the gods used the dodecahedron to create the Universe. For the storyteller, the dodecahedron so developed would represent the entire fictional world within which her/his story takes place. We have something that no longer represents just an element of the fictional construct but one that contains the entire imagined world of any story.

Now let's go back to the step just before we joined the two halves of the dodecahedron. Remember that when viewed from inside, the story progression arrow on the far side of the dodecahedron of Figure 6-4 reversed direction even though we'd created all the pentagons to be identical. Also, the central pentagon of that far side pointed down instead of up. This would lead one to believe that the initial plot pentagon, with its associated premise, represented just the story told from the protagonist's perspective. If the opposite pentagon, the one in the other half of the dodecahedron that points downwards and turns backwards in time, were to represent the story as seen from the antagonist's perspective, viewing it from this orientation would reverse everything and change the nature of the story altogether, from the premise up. We might even say that the antagonist would then become the protagonist. This is a profound revelation and says as much about conflict in the real world as it does about conflict in Story Land. This would illustrate why perspective, defined as point-of-view in fiction, is so important to meaning in a story. Each of us is the point-of-view character in our own life, just as we are the heroes of our own life stories.

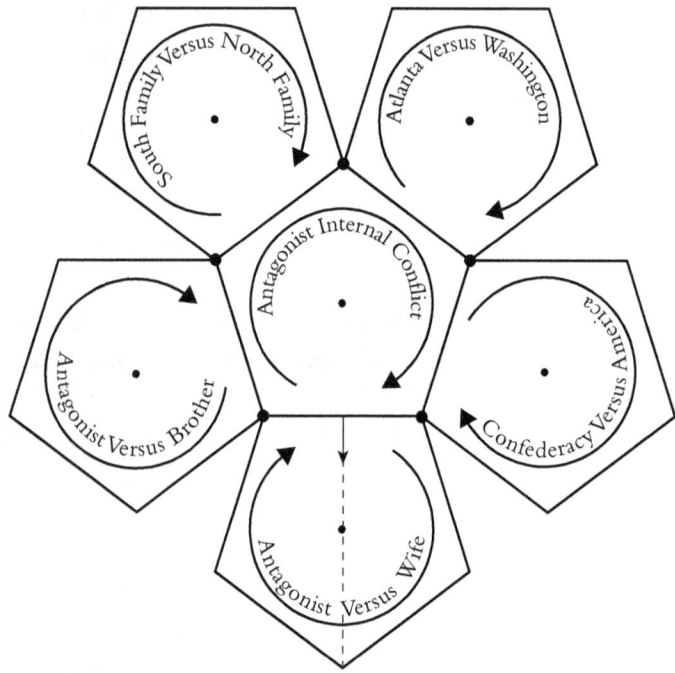

Figure 6-6 Antagonist Sub-Plot Diagram

I have again created a sub-plot pentagon, Figure 6-6, this time for the antagonist of the Civil War story previously sketch out in Chapter 2. This is really a superficial treatment, and I did it by simply rotating 180 degrees the protagonist sub-plot pentagon of Figure 6-2 and reversing the stated order of the conflicts. Still, I believe looking at it from this perspective illustrates how the nature of the story has changed. Of course, any plot pentagon in the dodecahedron of the Civil War story could be used as the point-of-view pentagon. It then becomes a much different story.

The Philosopher's Stone

If we take this one step further, the most basic premise is: Good versus Evil. And then Murray Stein, a Jungian analyst, author and lecturer, has a curious perspective on the subject: "Perhaps evil is only the absence of good, or merely the product of point of view." [Murray Stein, *Jung on Evil*, page 7] Furthermore, Jung has this to say on the subject of archetypes of the Collective Unconscious:

In itself, an archetype is neither good nor evil. It is morally neutral, like the gods of antiquity, and becomes good or evil only by contact with the conscious mind, or else a paradoxical mixture of both. [Jung, *The Spirit in Man, Art, and Literature,* page 104]

We might conclude from this that moral judgment comes solely from perspective. The story's point-of-view determines the orientation of the story dodecahedron when the reader reads the story. Of course, the protagonist's story can be told from the antagonist's point of view. A marvelous example of this is the movie *Amadeus*, staring Tom Hulce as Mozart (protagonist) and F. Murray Abraham as Salieri (antagonist). Salieri, the narrator of the story, is an old man looking back on his life and friendship with Mozart with considerable bitterness.

We also see that we could have told the story with one of the other twelve pentagons as the point-of-view. If so, it would have been much different, and this begs the question: Where is the narrator of this story in this expanded three-dimensional picture? Identifying the position of the narrator within this geometric structure could help limit all these alternatives. A few paragraphs back, I promised to find a place for him/her/it.

Just as with the bindu/premise, which resides in the center of the pentagon, the narrator must reside in the geometric center of the dodecahedron and must enter the dodecahedron from the point-of-view pentagon to get the right perspective on the story. She/he/it is located in this fictional world and is the voice that tells this story and describes the dramatic events that occur within it. The narrator is the channeler of the story. If we viewed the story dodecahedron as an orchestra playing a symphony, the narrator would be the conductor. And one might well wonder how the narrator goes about her/his/its business and also about her/his/its relationship with the author. To uncover that kinship, we'll have to look into Active Imagination, which we'll do in the next chapter.

Be patient. We're getting there.

Now we have a geometric representation of the entire story. It consists of a central conflict and associated subplots, all combined, interrelated and symbolized as a dodecahedron. We can envision a sphere enclosing the dodecahedron (the same sphere that cost Hippasus his life) that includes all twenty of its vertices. This is analogous to the circle in the two-dimensional pentagon. In the pentagon, the circle represented the Ouroboros, the dragon that eats its own tail. What might this sphere, as a three-dimensional extension of these individual circles, represent?

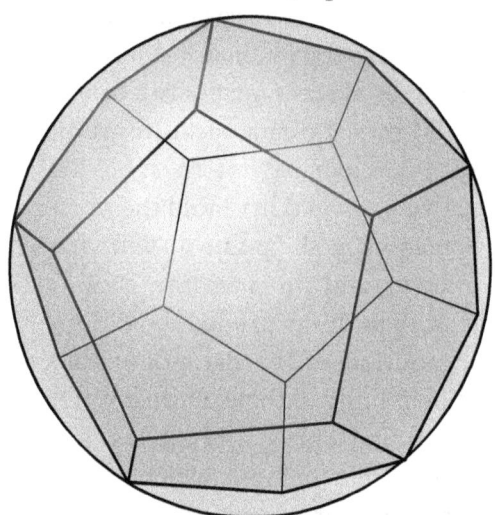

Figure 6-7 Dodecahedron Inside a Sphere
- The Philosopher's Stone

It might not be so easy to prove geometrically, but intuitively we can see that such a sphere would also contain every point in every circle, all the Ouroboroses, about all twelve pentagons. This sphere would represent something that contains the entire

The Philosopher's Stone

Universe and, since it also contains all twelve dragons, be fierce and mysterious beyond imagining. No one knows for certain what the Pythagoreans believed the sphere represented, but the only concept that seems to fit is God. Although it was not highly publicized, ancient Greek religion had a monotheistic element. The father of all gods and mankind was Zeus, who ruled from Mt. Olympus. The Greeks had a saying: "All things are ultimately Zeus." It would seem that this sphere that encloses the dodecahedron would have represented, to the Pythagoreans, Olympian Zeus.

We must realize that, for our purposes, this is a fictional world and not the "real" one. Who is our creator? Of course, it's all inside the author's psyche. The narrator in the geometric center of the dodecahedron would then be the vehicle for channeling the author's Collective Unconscious as the metaphorical god of this fictional universe in the Land of Story.

★

I'm not suggesting the author construct his/her story with all this in mind. However, this geometric approach to story structure, in the tradition of the Pythagoreans and the alchemical efforts of Sir Isaac Newton, demonstrates not only its complexity and interconnectedness, but also its central unity. The fact that each pentagon expands infinitely outward and shrinks infinitely inward provides the spiritual and psychological dimensions the story must have to become fully realized in the hands of the author.

All stories have as structure the assemblage of plot and subplot pentagons that form the dodecahedron. Storytelling is a natural part of being human, and it can be a part of the process that leads us to become more fully human and our natural selves. For those who choose to follow such a path, this dodecahedron must be our guiding symbol and the mechanism of our enlightenment. It provides not only the divine form to guide us, but simultaneously provides the way to becoming individuated, i.e., worthy.

The writing of a novel or script is the creation of a fictional world, just as God created Earth and the Universe. We aren't as

Story Alchemy

talented, and indeed we are using materials he created, including the lives of human beings. It's a humbling realization. We pull this material, these fictional characters' lives, from within our own psyche, our Collective Unconscious where the Divine World resides. The stories we write we find within us, or possibly, they find us. Many can't quit writing. We must write to be who we are. We are driven. Many writers talk of the writing process as being one of channeling rather than creation. It's as if the story already exists, has always existed, and we are only giving it voice. This is the nature of the fictional world revealed through storytelling.

I am not going to pretend that I understand all that this symbol has to tell us. I have just scratched the surface in decoding it. Perhaps it speaks to each of us differently, providing inspiration and insight appropriate to our needs and talent. It does speak to me, and in a loud voice. Conceivably, it'll speak to you also, possibly in a different language and with unique revelations divergent from my own.

This is the end of our search. The plot dodecahedron incased in the sphere is a three-dimensional divine object, proclaimed so by the Pythagoreans and kept secret under threat of death. It provides a complete view of story structure, the fictional world, and insight into the nature of storytelling. It contains pretty much everything generic that can be said about the structure of storytelling, just as Newton's Laws of Motion contained methods for the prediction of flight dynamics. It provides a temple for the construction of all stories. As such, it is the Philosopher's Stone.

It appears that this storytelling device is what Jorge Luis Borges called the aleph. Borges' character in his story "The Aleph" defines it as: "...one of the points in space that contain all points." Borges' aleph has its origin as the first letter of the Hebrew alphabet, and as such it is the letter that begets all other letters, that beget all words. We might infer that it also begets all stories in the Collective Unconscious. Borges also says: "...a Persian mystic speaks of a bird that somehow is all birds." Surely, that is our Philosopher's Stone for storytelling. It contains the

The Philosopher's Stone

essence of all stories. The aleph and the bindu are similar. Both are the source from which all subsequent actions proceed.

Whatever the importance of these peripheral revelations, we've found the object of our search. Alchemists kept such knowledge secret. They felt it shouldn't fall into the hands of the undeserving. We have gone into Chaos, discovered the prima materia, and turned it into story — a chaos-of-words to story, a divine narrative that lives on in the psyches of the world.

Now, to wield the Stone, we must become worthy.

CHAPTER 7 Becoming Worthy

In 1913, Carl Jung broke with Sigmund Freud. They had been colleagues for six years, and the schism formed over what Jung believed was Freud's overemphasis on sex and limited view of the Unconscious. At the time of the split, Jung started having visions, hearing voices and seeing beings within his own psyche that seemed autonomous. He believed he was going insane, or as he termed it, "doing a schizophrenia." Rather than running from what was going on inside himself, he decided to confront these psychic entities and see where they took him. He realized that his patients were experiencing the same phenomenon because he recognized their symptoms in himself, and thought that if he couldn't deal with this psychic material, he couldn't ask his patients to either. Thus began the many years of his own experience with these visions and voices, the outgrowth of which was the process he came to call Active Imagination. He documented his experience in *The Red Book*, which has only recently (2009) been published.

Back in Chapter 5 when I provided Mary Shelley's description of how she came up with the idea for *Frankenstein*, in addition to describing the experience of contacting the Collective Unconscious, I was also preparing you for Active Imagination. Mary used the method intuitively and to great effect. She had

Becoming Worthy

unknowingly prepared herself for a psychic experience by discussing the reanimation of dead tissue with Percy Shelly and Lord Byron. This discussion continued late into the evening and even past the witching hour. Let's revisit Mary's initial words about the psychic state she was in when her idea came to her:

> *When I placed my head on the pillow, I did not sleep, nor could I be said to think. My imagination, unbidden, possessed and guided me, gifting the successive images that arose in my mind with a vividness far beyond the usual bounds of reverie. I saw—with shut eyes, but acute mental vision—I saw...*

She did not think or sleep but slipped into an imaginative state. She had cleared away her psychic space and let come what may. But she also had been actively trying to come up with a ghost story. Just before sleep she was "possessed" by her imagination. She was given a series of vivid images that terrorized her. We need a process that will replicate Mary's situation and actions and yield results on demand. This process is Jung's Active Imagination.

Back in Chapter 2, when I gave directions on how to develop an initial concept for a story, i.e., find the prima materia, I was seducing you into this whole process by suggesting you look at an image that came with your idea and concentrate on that image until it animated. Then you looked for conflict between the characters that inhabited your story. These seemingly benign visualization techniques constitute, as we have seen with Mary Shelley's example, the initial stages of Active Imagination. Jungian therapists teach Active Imagination to help patients integrate problematic psychic material, internal conflicts, from the Unconscious into Consciousness.

We will be using Active Imagination to assist us with storytelling, but we didn't develop our Philosopher's Stone for nothing. It provides us with one type of preparation when we plan to create a new story: structure. And we didn't select that structure, practically a template, arbitrarily. We used what some of the greatest storytellers of all time knew about story. Active

Imagination provides us with a technique for conjuring our story from within our Subconscious, and we will use its process in conjunction with our Philosopher's Stone.

Mary Shelly fell into Active Imagination intuitively. Carl Jung was dragged into it by his own autonomous psychic entities. We're not so lucky. How can we learn Active Imagination? Is it possible to enter such a creative psychic state at will? Luckily, Jung describes this process in detail at various points throughout his *Collected Works*. All his ideas on Active Imagination have been provided in a single book titled, *Jung on Active Imagination*, edited by Joan Chodorow. The following is his best description of the process [pages 167/8]. (The original source for the material is Jung's *Mysterium Coniunctionis*, paragraph 706):

This process [Active Imagination] *can... take place spontaneously or be artificially induced. In the latter case you choose a dream, or some other fantasy-image, and concentrate on it by simply catching hold of it and looking at it. You can also use a bad mood as a starting-point, and then try to find out what sort of fantasy-image it will produce, or what image expresses this mood. You then fix this image in the mind by concentrating your attention. Usually it will alter, as the mere fact of contemplating it animates it.*

This is a marvelously detailed description of the initial process. The notion that it will spontaneously animate if you contemplate it, although it may seem mundane, is quite profound for anyone who has attempted the process and has run into trouble getting it to work. Jung continues:

The alterations must be carefully noted down all the time, for they reflect the psychic processes in the unconscious background, which appear in the form of images consisting of conscious memory material. In this way conscious and unconscious are united, just as a waterfall connects above and below. A chain of fantasy ideas develops and gradually takes on a dramatic character: the passive process becomes an action.

For someone trying to come up with an idea for writing a

Becoming Worthy

novel or screenplay, this is like hearing the voice of the prophet. There's more:

> At first it consists of projected figures, and these images are observed like scenes in the theatre. In other words, you dream with open eyes. As a rule there is a marked tendency simply to enjoy this interior entertainment and to leave it at that. Then, of course, there is no real progress but only endless variations on the same theme, which is not the point of the exercise at all.

This is quite an analogy for someone trying to write fiction. It gets directly at the process. I might add that simply to be entertained isn't the point of writing fiction either. The author must be emotionally engaged. The point of fiction is to fully develop the central conflict and resolve it. Jung continues:

> What is enacted on the stage still remains a background process; it does not move the observer in any way, and the less it moves him the smaller will be the cathartic effect of this private theatre. The piece that is being played does not want merely to be watched impartially, it wants to compel his participation. If the observer understands that his own drama is being performed on this inner stage, he cannot remain indifferent to the plot and its denouement. He will notice, as the actors appear one by one and the plot thickens, that they all have some purposeful relationship to his conscious situation, that he is being addressed by the unconscious, and that it causes these fantasy-images to appear before him. He therefore feels compelled, or is encouraged by his analyst, to take part in the play and, instead of just sitting in a theatre, really have it out with his alter ego. For nothing in us ever remains quite uncontradicted, and consciousness can take up no position which will not call up, somewhere in the dark corners of the psyche, a negation or a compensatory effect, approval or resentment.

It's as if Jung is speaking directly to the author here. He even couches his argument in the lingo of storytelling. This beehive of conflict is a goldmine for an author. Remember that Mary Shelley's vision terrified her, an indication that she wasn't "watching impartially." She was fully emotionally involved, if only as a viewer of the action. One last paragraph from Jung, and it contains bad news, or perhaps really good news, depending on how you look at it:

> This process of coming to terms with the Other in us is well worth while, because in this way we get to know aspects of our nature which we would not allow anybody else to show us and which we ourselves would never have admitted. It is very important to fix this whole procedure in writing at the time of its occurrence, for you then have ocular evidence that will effectively counteract the ever-ready tendency to self-deception. A running commentary is absolutely necessary in dealing with the shadow, because otherwise its actuality cannot be fixed. Only in this painful way is it possible to gain a positive insight into the complex nature of one's own personality.

The bad news is, "...in this way we get to know aspects of our nature which we would not allow anybody else to show us and which we ourselves would never have admitted." We learn about ourselves from the stories we select to write, and this isn't a pretty picture. What interests us says a lot about our own psychic makeup. We rarely associate ourselves with our characters literally, nor would we want others to equate us with them. Think of Steven King. But our readers do, perhaps not in a totally literal sense, but they do. Storytelling, particularly fiction, gets to the inner workings of the author's psyche, and our readers instinctively know that these stories we tell are an indelible part of ourselves. But then these stories are a part of the reader's psychic makeup also, or they wouldn't be interested in reading them.

The one thing we should always remember is that we are never isolated from the creative process. It is always a therapeutic process of internal discovery and reconciliation. However, the news is not always good. We can activate repressed internal conflicts, and troublesome content from the Unconscious can flood Consciousness. Some of us are more susceptible to this than are others. It depends to a large extent on how much we've suppressed and repressed and the nature of that psychic material,

Becoming Worthy

i.e., the depth of the trauma, that created the Shadow and the way it is connected to the archetypes of the Collective Unconscious.

Here's another way of looking at what we're going to do. Normally your center of awareness is pointed forward. You go about your daily tasks with your awareness facing the world. What I'm now asking you to do, and will give you some tools to help accomplish, is to turn your awareness around so that it's facing backward staring directly at your Unconscious, but only during creative writing sessions. Graphically, it looks like this:

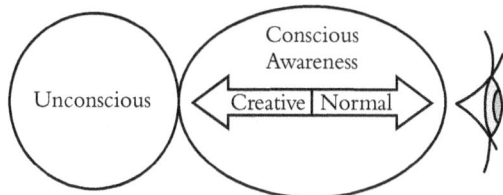

Figure 7-1 Direction of Awareness

To me as a layman, the definition of at least one type of insanity is a psyche within which awareness uncontrollably points inward toward the Unconscious instead of outward toward the real world. I assume that was Jung's problem when he started hearing voices and seeing visions. In such an inward configuration during daily activity, awareness can't distinguish what is actually happening versus what is going on inside this hidden psychic world as it is projected onto the perception of reality. In the beginning of this book, I warned that this method carries certain risks. You'll have to decide for yourself if you want to take that risk. If you run into trouble, you may need to spend some time with a Jungian therapist. We can also cultivate relationships with psychic forces buried deep within us that don't deserve a voice. It's up to the author to differentiate between those who should and those who shouldn't be turned loose upon the world.

Jung found that when using Active Imagination successfully, we build a bridge from Consciousness into the Unconscious, both the Shadow and the Collective, that facilitates and regulates the exchange of information, integrates material from it into

Story Alchemy

Consciousness, and makes the individual both more functional and individuated. This bridge, which the patient develops during Active Imagination sessions, Jung termed the Transcendent Function. It is the outgrowth of the process and what enables the patient to better function in the real world and within his/her own psyche.

Jung wasn't the first to practice such a therapeutic technique, perhaps the first to do so consciously, but others had been at it unconsciously for millennia. Jung studied the written works of the alchemists for decades and noticed similarities to his own experience. Jungians today still study the writing of the alchemists to learn more about the Transcendent Function. The book, *The Transcendent Function* by Jeffrey C. Miller, describes that process. Here's what Miller has to say about Alchemy:

Alchemy was concerned with creating qualitative changes in substances, specifically transforming base metals into gold or silver. Its importance to [depth psychology] *lies in its conviction that "outer" in the substances corresponded with "inner" changes in the alchemist's psyche; as the alchemical endeavor proceeds, transformation occurs in both the alchemist and the substance. Indeed, some would say that the transformation of the alchemist is the true focus of alchemy...*

...

Alchemy holds that subject and object, indeed all opposites, are joined in an unseen way by a universal process or substance, called the lapis, which imbues all creation, even the human mind and body. [Miller, *The Transcendent Function*, page 123]

This "lapis" (Latin for "stone") is what Jung called the Transcendent Function. What is interesting for the author is that she/he is engaged in a process quite similar to that of the alchemist. When we write, we are working on something viewed as external: the novel, screenplay, etc. The author is joining opposites, the protagonist and antagonist, and resolving their conflict. During the writing process, authors focus on perfecting the work, but the process involves pulling material from the Unconscious into

Becoming Worthy

Consciousness. In doing so, they are creating and using Jung's bridge, the Transcendent Function. Authors both improve their working relationship with their own Unconscious and create a work of art, their story.

To prepare for an Active Imagination session, Jung suggests the patient first do a little homework and go in with a purpose. In therapy, this is whatever is troubling the patient most. It can be something specific or as vague as a persistent bad feeling. For the author, I also suggest preparation, and that she/he go into Active Imagination with the purpose of learning something specific about the story. This can be a need to further develop the plot or to write a chapter or a scene. I'm assuming that the author has developed an idea as we talked about in Chapter 2. It can be just about anything.

But this is where I'm going to stop. We're not quite ready to enter psychic space. We need to know more about Jung's Active Imagination and how that process relates to our Philosopher's Stone. We also need to know how the actual story material we develop relates to the therapeutic process. All the material for your story, at least its heart and soul, most of the words, will come from the Unconscious. You will simultaneously experience a form of therapy because the processes are interrelated. You will, in some ways, be building Jung's Transcendent Function disguised as narrative storytelling. The story isn't the Transcendent Function precisely, but it will be akin to it, or maybe even more accurately a representation of it. One of many, actually. The thing to recognize is that you are cloaking your Active Imagination sessions as story construction sessions. The outgrowth of your sessions, once edited, will be your written work. It will be something about you, but not about you. You've disguised your Active Imagination session as writing fiction, and its product you've called a work of art.

This is nothing new. Every work of fiction is and always has been the product of disguised Active Imagination. It's just that authors didn't and don't realize it. What I'm doing is taking you another step, perhaps many steps, closer to hardcore Active

Story Alchemy

Imagination, and toward butting right up against the Unconscious. You will be aware, much more intensely aware, of the place from which the creative material is coming. Plus, it will change you.

For a Christian perspective on this, we turn to the non-canonical, but widely quoted by scholars, *Gospel of Thomas* (70): Jesus said, "If you bring forth what is within you, what you bring forth will save you. If you do not bring forth what is within you, what you do not bring forth will destroy you." This is the same as Jung's contention that what we suppress into the Shadow is unknowingly projected out into the world, and it's not pretty. It was suppressed for a reason, and that reason was that it was unacceptable to society. In a good portion of our own writing, we are bringing our forbidden impulses into the fictional world. They are disguised in daily life but still projected "out there" and help form our perceptions of people and events. We react to these mistaken perceptions and develop "blind spots" to our bad behavior. Once we come to terms with the unconscious content through writing, we can deal with it internally without allowing its destructive effect to be projected onto the real world. The suppressed content then has expression within fiction and is not acted upon. At least that's the theory.

Instead of mistakenly trying to resolve these internal issues in the real world, we are writing stories about them, just as the alchemist was perfecting himself while trying to create the Philosopher's Stone and the Elixir of Life. Your novel or screenplay will be proof of your striving for individuation. Your story will be the alchemist's gold which she/he transmuted from lead. By use of the author's Philosopher's Stone, the plot yantra/mandala and the dodecahedron, you will transform your prima materia and de-energize it by resolving your internal conflicts.

This process is forever a hall of mirrors. When it comes right down to it, this storytelling process isn't about story at all. It's about presiding over the resolution of conflicts between Consciousness and the Unconscious, both within you and your readers. That Philosopher's Stone for storytellers we just discovered has its origin within the psyche. One might say that the original Philosopher's Stone is about the psyche, and we've only developed a replica of it for storytelling. Our story will have the shape and contents of a Philosopher's Stone, but the psyche must be so configured to be psychologically healthy, to see clearly and understand the story. One might well imagine that this Philosopher's Stone is the basic structure of the psyche in the healthy state and describes psychic processes when it's working properly. This then is what we call being "worthy." Here's how we might describe this graphically:

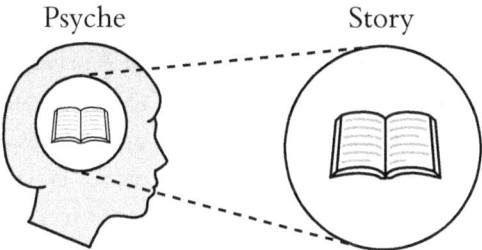

Figure 7-2 Story as a Psychic Mirror

Story creation is a process of looking into a mirror. We all have had the experience of cruising along with our story when we come to a difficult part that we just can't quite get right. We close our eyes and "look" within. We didn't realize it, but we were trying to see "back" into our psyche because we instinctively know that the creative material comes from some dark place within us. We project that material forward into our story. It's as if our awareness is a projector for the contents of the Unconscious.

Let's take a quick look at Jung's therapeutic process for creating the Transcendent Function. When you first read about it, you might get the feeling that the process seems familiar. Jung viewed the process of forming the Transcendent Function as one of bringing opposites that reside in Consciousness and the Unconscious into direct conflict so that contents from the Unconscious could be integrated into Consciousness. This is a process of conflict engagement and resolution. It has six steps but still seemingly fits our five-plot-point pentagon.

Story Alchemy

Here are Jung's steps as outlined by Miller, along with what I see as their corresponding points on our plot pentagon (see pages 21-28 of *The Transcendent Function*):

Artificially Inducing Unconscious Contents (AIUC) When the self-regulating nature of position/counter-position between Consciousness and the Unconscious breaks down, it's necessary to artificially induce interaction to restart the process. [In storytelling, this constitutes the Setup and Locking the Conflict. It corresponds to the Setup and Plot Point 1 on the plot pentagon. It puts the characters in motion.]

Producing Unconscious Material: Active Imagination (PUMAI) This is the initial stage in the mechanics of creating the Transcendent Function. Consciousness actively seeks out interaction with the Unconscious. It consists of finding the disturbing symptom (conflict) and diving into its core. [This is the process of the protagonist coming to terms with what the central conflict is all about, and corresponds to the action along the line between PP1 – PP2.]

Utilizing Unconscious Material: Creative Formulation and Understanding (CF&U) This is where Consciousness struggles to understand the content from the Unconscious. [In storytelling this is the point where the protagonist fully understands the conflict, what she/he's up against. This is PP2, and includes the action along the line between PP2 – PP3.]

Relation of Ego to Unconscious: Bringing together the Opposites (BTO) Jung states: "At this stage it is no longer the unconscious that takes the lead, but the ego". [The first part of this step is a reversal in the conflict, PP3. The action forced by the ego (Consciousness) occurs between PP3 – PP4.]

Final Result: Dialogue Creating Emergence of the Third (DCET) The Transcendent Function comes fully into being through a conversation between Consciousness and the Unconscious. [The protagonist finally makes a decision as to how he/she will approach the antagonist. This decision point is PP4. This precipitates the prolonged struggle (conversation) that occurs between PP4 – PP5.]

Closing Passages: Liberation and the Courage to be Oneself (LCO) Functional to-and-fro arguments as permitted now by the creation of the Transcendent Function. [The conflict is finally resolved at PP5. What follows from PP5 – PP1 is the Denouement, which is a brief presentation of the results of the conflict. This then brings us back to where we started, normal life.]

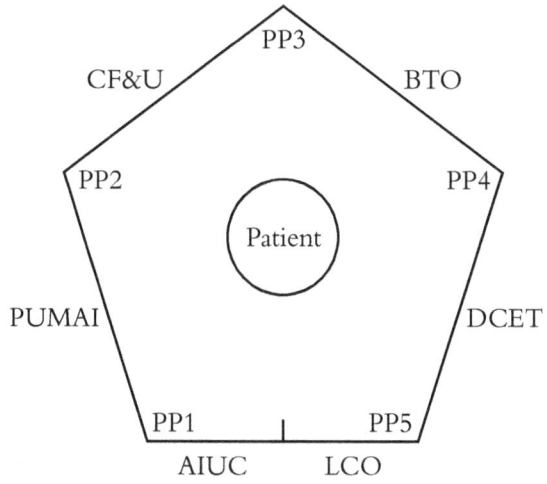

Figure 7-3 Jung's Active Imagination as a Pentagon

It seems that both the plotting process for storytelling and the structure of Jungian psychotherapy are meditations on conflict and directions on how to achieve resolution. What is so surprising is how well Jungian psychology explains the author's process. It seems that, in developing our own theory of storytelling, we've run directly into Jung's process of individuation. A patient's internal conflicts manifest and get resolved through therapy, a process that leads to individuation if resolved successfully. In Jungian psychology, the patient (the conflicted self) would be at the center of a therapeutic pentagon, whereas in storytelling the premise, conflict incarnate, occupies that spot. This means that the author is the patient when writing fiction. The author is always struggling with an internal conflict that is resolved through storytelling.

★

Now that we've come this far down the road to good storytelling, let's take a really cynical look at what we've done. So what if the conflict is resolved? Shouldn't something more profound about the protagonist be happening? How does this relate to consciousness raising? And, what does this really tell us about the author becoming worthy? A lot of novels, plays and movies are built around conflict, probably have all these plot points, and many still suck. How do we get to a place where it all means something, possibly even something profound?

We've already addressed this, but now we'll expand upon it. Meaning comes from theme. To explore theme properly, both sides of the argument must be reasonably presented, and that argument will become the vise that puts the squeeze on theme and results in meaning. Let's redraw Figure 2-1 and make it more graphically telling:

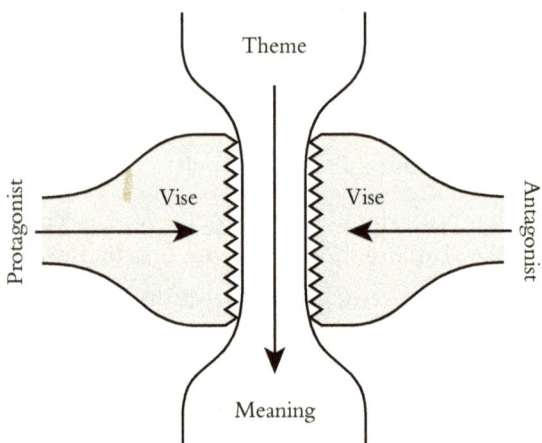

Figure 7-4 Conflict Squeezing Theme Yields Meaning

Conflict is a mechanism for exploring theme. If the antagonist doesn't have a reasoned position relative to the theme, the conflict becomes one-sided. A one-sided vise doesn't work.

To illustrate that conflict, in and of itself, isn't theme, consider the case where the protagonist loses the conflict but gains wisdom in the process. Perhaps when the protagonist went through the agony of choice, she/he came to the realization that she/he didn't want to win, that they were wrong. They realized that the higher road was in losing. In doing so, they transcended the conflict and became a better person. She/he became enlightened. In losing the conflict, the protagonist has saved her/his own soul. Conflict is about winning or losing; becoming worthy is about enlightenment; theme processing leads to enlightenment, individuation, worthiness. Conflict without theme is story without meaning. The story has no soul.

Consider the movie, *Kramer vs Kramer*. Following a divorce, the mother wins custody of their child, but in the end, she gives the little boy back to her ex-husband because the mother realizes that he will be better off with his father. She has transcended the conflict through love for her child and respect for the father — and the realization, which hurts the most, of her own limitations as a mother.

The best way to look at what happens as a result of conflict and its resolution is through the lens of a mandala. The Hindu and Buddhist traditions teach "the five types of deep awareness," with a different Buddha representing each of the five awarenesses. I mentioned these awarenesses back in Chapter 4, but briefly. Now we must fully develop the concept. We can adapt some of this Eastern philosophy without pulling too heavily on their traditions by insisting that the protagonist learn something profound at each step, i.e., plot point, of his/her journey through Storyland. These are the milestones that occur when the connection between conflict and theme surface dramatically. You might call the Five Types of Deep Awareness a parallel pentagon that charts the major learning experience of the protagonist. See Figure 7-5. The interaction between the basic natures of each plot point, together with the theme, fully develops the story's philosophical content.

Up until now, we've viewed each plot point as an event confronted by the protagonist, but we can also view each as a learning experience, something that will help her/him overcome the obstacles presented by the central conflict. Each of the five plot points presents the protagonist with a different manifestation of the same, ever escalating, central conflict, but each also provides an opportunity to learn, to become wiser. In writing about the protagonist's struggles and increasing awareness, the author, by becoming emotionally and intellectually involved, also becomes enlightened. The nature of the theme, indelibly etched in the central conflict, determines the makeup of the consciousness-raising achieved by both author and protagonist.

To help envision how enlightenment results from theme under the flames of conflict, we place the author as the Ouroboros, the circling dragon, and the five theme plot points as teachings that arrive as different aspects of the conflict as experienced by the protagonist.

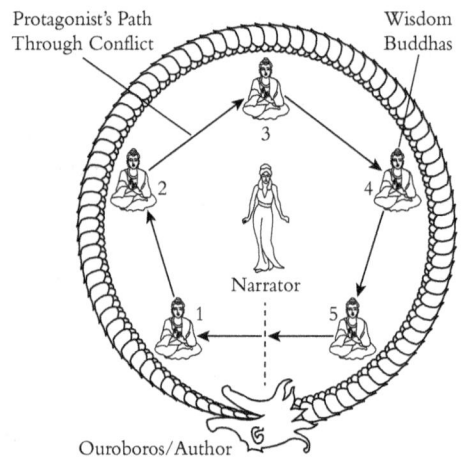

Figure 7-5 The Five Types of Deep Awareness

The five wisdom Buddhas embody the progress of enlightenment. The protagonist then experiences the following five teachings at the five plot points: (1) conflict recognition, (2) experiences conflict's true nature, (3) withstands the full conflict, (4) recognition of resolution, (5) enforcing the resolution. What is crucial is that each of these five teachings originates in the theme as part of the central conflict. All the while, of course, we have the ever-circling Ouroboros, which is the author. Shown in the form of a mandala, the theme plot pentagon looks like that in Figure 7-5. Theme enters from the center with the narrator's premise and point of view, and then the protagonist progresses around the wisdom pentagon as the Ouroboros/author starts its/his cycle about the mechanism. The protagonist undergoes the five steps to gain full theme awareness.

What proof can I offer that psychotherapy/writing/Active Imagination have done anything to help me along the path to individuation, i.e., becoming worthy? Sometime in early 2012, two years into Active Imagination, I had a dream that concerned me quite a lot. I avoided telling about it on my blog, but it stuck with me, so eventually I did. Here's what I wrote the night of the dream:

> *I dreamed that I was with a bunch of people who were giving me their condolences. I didn't exactly understand why. We were outside walking, and when we started to cross the street, I saw something lying in the gutter among leaves and other debris. It was a body, stripped of clothing, and when I went to see who it was, my friends tried to stop me, but I walked over to it anyway. It was lying under the front end of a parked car. The car hadn't run over it. It was just lying there dead and discarded. By then I realized that it was me, my body. I felt great affection for it, and I was heartbroken that I was dead. I took a hold of my hand and moved my body around a bit, but I was dead. Dead and just simply discarded there at the side of the street. In the gutter. Under a car.*
>
> *But I had a new body and my friends wanted me to move on. I went into a home and went to the bathroom mirror to see what my new body looked like. I was surprised. I looked a little like a friend I had when I was in high school fifty-three years ago. I was not pleased, but at least I didn't look horrible. It wasn't as if I was reincarnated but more like I had just received a new body to replace the old one. It was not a traumatizing dream but not very pleasant either.*

This dream was undoubtedly a result of my Active Imagination sessions. If you remember, the Ouroboros is the dragon that eats its own tail, therefore, constantly dying and resurrecting itself. Here's what Jung says of the Ouroboros:

> In the age-old image of the [o]uroboros lies the thought of devouring oneself and turning oneself into a circulator process, for it was clear to the more astute alchemists that the prima materia of the art was man himself. The uroboros is a dramatic symbol for the integration and assimilation of the opposite, i.e., of the shadow. This "feed-back" process is at the same time a symbol of immortality, since it is said of the uroboros that he slays himself and brings himself to life, fertilizes himself and gives birth to himself. He symbolizes the One, who proceeds from the clash of opposites, and he therefore constitutes the secret of the prima materia which, as a projection, unquestionably stems from man's unconscious. [*Mysterium Coniunctionis*, page 365, para 513]

By "he slays himself," Jung means the repression and suppression of some of our natural tendencies that fall into the Shadow, and by "brings himself to life" Jung refers to the therapeutic process of bringing the contents of the Shadow back up into consciousness. In doing this, we become somewhat of a different person, which he describes as giving birth to ourselves anew as the One. And as in my dream, we are perhaps not as "beautiful" as we were before because we've absorbed some of our less favorable characteristics that we'd previously discarded/repressed to become civilized. The new, or reborn person, he considers individuated. What the individuated person has gained that makes him so different is the Transcendent Function, which is the functional bridge that enables Consciousness to interact successfully and continually with the Unconscious and integrate its contents.

My dream seems to have been a direct result of the process I was using to write a vampire novel. I'm not very conscientious about documenting my dreams. I don't even make much of an attempt to remember them. It's a laborious process about which I've become complacent. But this one dream, which had a major emotional impact, I finally realized, is indicative of what was

Becoming Worthy

going on within me at the time and deserved to be documented. When writing of the alchemists, Marie-Louise von Franz, who worked with Jung for twenty-eight years, put it this way:

> *The underlying, not consciously realized thought is that if one gets deeper into psychology, one will have to give up all one's present weltanschauung* [comprehensive world view], *thoughts, and occupations. Thus people feel threatened — and in a way they are right, they are threatened, because if they get in touch with their own depth, their former frame of life will collapse. Thus, in that form, medicine has a primarily destructive effect on the former framework of the personality's rational consciousness. Everybody knows that he or she has to be drowned and lie like a corpse at the bottom of the green and white water before being resurrected, but this effect goes further and ultimately cures the person.* [*Alchemical Active Imagination*, pages 56/7]

It "cures" the person, but not before she/he has suffered a symbolic death and their life completely upturned, as mine had been. The psychic equivalent was my death and rebirth, which I experienced in my dream. If you pursue this creative process, it could happen to you. If you've been writing for quite a while, it has probably already worked at least some of its dirt on you, and you've ended up better for it, at least in some ways.

In therapy, the psychotherapist is an advisor that facilitates the process, providing the patient with the crucial treatment and information needed to help create the Transcendent Function and negotiate the resolution of the internal conflict. In storytelling, frequently the protagonist also has such an advisor, and that person is, interestingly enough, called the thematic character because she/he is there to teach the protagonist how to engage the antagonist. In the first *Star Wars* movie, the thematic character is Obi-Wan Kenobi, who teaches Luke Skywalker about the Force. In the second, it's Yoda, who trains Luke to be a Jedi Knight. In James Cameron's movie *Titanic*, Jack tells Rose about freedom and helps her find the courage to break free from family shackles. Thematic characters pop up naturally as a part of the creative process. This is particularly true of coming-of-age stories where the protagonist has a lot to learn to solve the predicament she/he is in.

Learning Active Imagination is a process, a skill we develop over time — days, months, years. We come into it with a certain skill level because it is a natural process. Learning all the details of practicing Active Imagination makes it more effective and controllable, hopefully. I'm much more proficient than I was when I first started even though I'd been writing for decades. I've also noticed that it's improved my creative skill during editing, by virtue of the Transcendent Function, no doubt. Don't be disappointed if the process doesn't seem very effective at first. You'll work into it. The initial part of becoming worthy is undoubtedly about the Shadow, but the bigger picture is about building that additional part of the Transcendent Function that will connect Consciousness with not only the Shadow but also the Collective Unconscious.

★

Okay, we know what being worthy is all about, and we're ready to get the show on the road. Are we supposed to go inside the Philosopher's Stone? But it's a formidable, solid object with no door. Our pilgrimage has led us to a sacred site which is in itself another unsolvable mystery. Maybe it was just a bowling ball all along and isn't as useful as we thought. We have a meditation technique, a tradition, called Active Imagination, but how does it work with the Stone? Seems hopeless.

Don't walk away just yet. Since the Unconscious has brought us this far along the road to achieving our goal, perhaps it can help find a way inside. And we really do have to get in because no way can we accomplish anything from outside. We have to be intimately involved with the Philosopher's Stone. I had some strange experiences when I first started practicing Active Imagination that just might be able to help. Perhaps, I have a key that opens this thing.

In a scene in the 1956 classic movie *Forbidden Planet*, the main characters pass through a pentagonal-shaped door and take a shuttle to another part of the planet to witness the technological marvels of an ancient but extinct alien civilization called the Krell. The circular tunnel they negotiate while in the shuttle has a series of lights that extend far off into the distance where they travel. This tunnel is like a track into the center of a bindu, particularly after getting to it through a pentagonal-shaped door that could represent our plot pentagon. When they reach their destination, they are inside a wondrous machine that occupies four-hundred square miles and goes about its business unaided without any human or alien guidance, much as the Collective Unconscious goes about its business without the individual's awareness.

Figure 7-6 *Forbidden Planet* Shuttle

This alien machine is powered by an energy source, as is our bindu, in the very center of the planet that is of almost infinite capacity. It drove the Krell's advanced civilization and enabled them to instantaneously create anything that their minds could imagine and project it into the real world. This is what authors do. We need an entrance to our own energy center, and that plot pentagon might provide a clue to the location of a door.

CHAPTER 8 The Iris of Time

The bad news is we don't have a shuttle. The good news is we do, however, have a pentagonal shape that we just might be able to use as a door. Plus, we have a bridge, the Transcendent Function. When I first started Active Imagination, I had a dream, which I will now relay in detail. The date was May 4, 2010:

This morning I had a dream that a young woman came to me bearing a key in her left hand. She came to me out on a balcony, I believe, but she walked up to a cabinet where she left the key. I'm not sure where she went. The next thing I remember is that I retrieved the key and walked back into the room from the balcony. It was much like a living room, but no one was inside. I walked through the room, as if I knew where I was going, and through an archway. The adjoining room was small except that the far wall was entirely a large mechanism, much like a big vault in a bank. Somehow, the key was supposed to unlock this large structure. I have no idea what was on the other side.

The young woman was of average height, possibly blond, or light brown hair, and thin. She wore a white-laced dress, belted about the waist. Perhaps she is a facilitator of some sort. She said nothing to me and did not acknowledge me, although she seemed to be there for my benefit.

What intrigued me about this dream were, yes of course the woman but also, the key and the mechanism. The very next night,

The Iris of Time

May 5th, I had an unusual vision just before sleep. Here's what I wrote in my journal:

I had just turned out the light to go to sleep, no more than five minutes, when suddenly a man popped through the darkness, as if through a door in front of me, and came toward me but walked rapidly on past. He was young, maybe thirty-five, dark hair, well-dressed. I believe he spoke as he came through the door, but actually I'm not sure there was a door there at all, maybe just darkness. It was all over in a flash and was so totally unexpected. The young man's mood was pleasant but not jovial. I have the impression that he just might be British. [Actually probably the Greek god Hermes, who transgresses boundaries and is guide of souls in the Underworld.]

At first, I didn't associate the dream of the woman with the key with this unusual vision just before sleep. They seemed two separate and unconnected events. Then a few days later, I was talking to my son, and I mentioned the vision I'd had at the very beginning of my excursion through Active Imagination, where the character burst through the darkness and swept past me. I told my son that I associated the location, where the man in my vision had come from, with the mechanism in my dream of May 4th. I compared it to the TV series *Stargate*, where people returning from other worlds enter through a stargate, which is an entrance to a wormhole. An iris that opens and closes, thus permitting or preventing entry, covers the stargate. During the conversation, it became obvious to me that I'd already solved the puzzle and didn't realize it. I then named my mechanism the Iris of Time, a phrase I invented while writing a book on how Mary Shelley came up with the idea for *Frankenstein*. But of what use was this mechanism? I didn't have a purpose for it. I then read a passage in a book that enabled me to put it all together:

...[human beings] *do have important responsibilities in the consecration of the* [sacred] *space and in the stewardship of its boundaries. Whether the space was directly generated by a hierophantic event or the result of the application of traditional techniques for provoking a sign, the*

101

creation of an enclosure, a clear boundary between the two realms, was always important. [Robert L. Moore, "Ritual, Sacred Space, and Healing," in *Liminality and Transitional Phenomena*, ed. by Nathan Schwartz-Salant and Murray Stein, page 16]

As Mircea Eliade put it:

The enclosure, wall, or circle of stones surrounding a sacred place — these are among the most ancient of known forms of man-made sanctuary. [*Patterns of Comparative Religions*, page 370]

My Unconscious was telling me how it wanted me to setup my Active Imagination sessions. It still took me a while to realize that the circular shape of the Iris suggested that it was a yantra/mandala. I'd been wondering how to meditate on my plot mandala, and here was the answer. I could use this circular mechanism, this yantra/mandala, as an entry point into psychic space when I conducted an Active Imagination session to generate material for my own writing. I had read that Jung said mandalas appear spontaneously during therapy. It had happened to me, and I didn't even realize it.

Something seemed to have guided me through all this, revealing bits and pieces of a process one element at a time, building up all the hardware required for the journey into the Land of Story. I view the entrance in the shape of a pentagon, much like the doors of the ancient Krell in *Forbidden Planet*.

Figure 8-1 Ancient Krell Doorway

The Iris of Time

Of course, our not-so-friendly dragon, the Ouroboros, circles the door, the plot pentagon. See Figure 8-2 below. When I enter, I envision the dragon to be turned clockwise so that she stimulates the appropriate portion of the plot pentagon. The Iris itself is like the circular leaf shutter of a camera, which opens as an ever-dilating pentagon/pentagram in the center, the expansion of the bindu. When it opens, I step through into the World of the Unconscious. In that way, I enter sacred space, and as such must be respectful of both how I enter and what I do there. Remember that the plot yantra is a mechanism with a sympathetic resonance for a certain portion of psychic energy related to storytelling. Even though this may appear in many ways to be similar to a therapy session, we don't have a therapist-in-waiting to direct our activities and keep us out of trouble. When Jung first developed Active Imagination, he was on his own too, but he was a psychiatrist. However, you won't be alone either. You'll just have to wait a bit to find out about this companion who will help you through this.

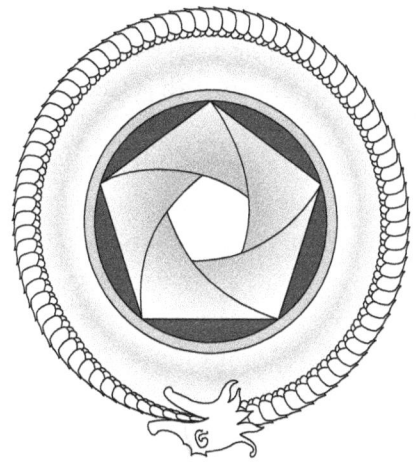

Figure 8-2 Iris of Time with Ouroboros

What's on the other side of the Iris of Time, this mechanism through which we're about to step? The first thing our feet touch is the bridge that we call the Transcendent Function. We don't have a tunnel or a shuttle, but we have that bridge. Of course, the Iris of Time is only one of twelve pentagons that make up the larger three-dimensional structure, the dodecahedron. When we step through the mechanism, we enter what I've rather provocatively called the Philosopher's Stone. This is a divine object and entering it must be accomplished with due respect and proper ritual. It's like entering a church. Lots of profane activity will go on inside, but the Bible also has its share of debauchery. Since it is a representation of at least a portion of the Unconscious, you'd expect it to be a fairly strange and frightening world. You won't be disappointed.

Why do I need the Iris of Time? Why not just jump right into Active Imagination? My answer is that I could, but just recognizing psychic space as a place to look for images or listen for voices isn't necessarily enough preparation for entry. Naming my entrance the "Iris of Time" and developing a ritual to get inside makes that sacred space specific, familiar and prepares me for the activity. It provides a demarcation line, a boundary that also gives me the first push into liminality by making me conscious of crossing a threshold and that I have entered an unusual psychic state. In doing so, we should treat that sacred boundary with the respect it deserves.

The value of trying to contact the Collective Unconscious through the Iris of Time is that it constitutes what we might call "liminal territory." Liminality is a transitional psychic state, the threshold between worlds. It is the twilight zone. Interestingly, it is the purview of Hermes. Since we are going to be speaking a lot about liminality, a concise definition as it applies to our subject matter is crucial. Murray Stein's definition is the best I've come across:

> *The English "liminality" comes from the Latin limen, meaning 'doorway' or 'threshold.' Entering a room or leaving it, one crosses a limen, and while there, in this borderline space, one is in liminality, if only for a half second.*
>
> *This Latin root has infiltrated psychology, where it is used to refer to the threshold between consciousness and the unconscious portions of the*

mind. So, the term "subliminal" refers to psychological territory below the threshold of conscious awareness. This threshold is crossed and recrossed in going to sleep and awakening, and in the twilight state between the two, again, is liminality. [In Midlife, page 8]

While we're within the Philosopher's Stone, we are straddling the boundary between consciousness and the unconscious, have a foot in each world, so we are in a state of liminality. When we enter Active Imagination just prior to sleep, during the night when we wake, or in the morning, we are at the threshold between the World of Dreams and that of reality, the zone between Consciousness and the Unconscious. In this state, we also tend to throw off our identities and are much more susceptible to taking on different ones, a good thing for writing fiction.

We can do much the same thing during the day while sitting alone in a room, but our biorhythms are configured differently, and we are not nearly so close to the Unconscious. I believe both situations have their advantages because in the daytime method, you face more toward the Consciousness side of the liminal zone, and in the nighttime technique, you are facing more toward the Unconscious side. Sometimes it's better with your intellect in the advantage, and at others, it's better for it to take a backseat to the Unconscious. Explore all the possibilities; just be aware of the differences and use them to your advantage.

I want to reinforce the fact that the act of crossing sacred boundaries carries with it the necessity of doing so with respect and procedure, a Code of Conduct, if you will. You're on a journey and entering a world where you quite literally do not belong. Your saving grace is that you are still tethered physically to the real world, a little like Ariadne's thread she provided Theseus when he enter the labyrinth so that he might find the way out, and it would serve you well to have an entry and exit method also. As Robert L. Moore says in an essay titled "Ritual, Sacred Space, and Healing":

The importance of the establishment and maintenance of the

Story Alchemy

boundaries of a sacred space can hardly be overemphasized. Not only does the boundary serve notice that entry into a radically different mode of human existence is near, but the recognition of and proper respect for the boundary is the sine qua non for a proper relationship to sacred space and the primary condition for being benefited and not harmed by contact with it. [*Liminality and Transitional Phenomena*, edited by Nathan Schwartz-Salant and Murray Stein, pages 16/7]

To satisfy these process requirements, I've identified an entity that I call the Keeper of the Gate, i.e, the Keeper of the Iris. Addressing the Keeper or simply acknowledging her puts me in contact with the psychic presence that accomplishes, hopefully, a safe transition. Also addressing all those within the Collective Unconscious, as well as my Shadow, with a few perfunctory words reinforces my own perception that this liminal psychic space contains entities that are "other." I'm preparing myself to meet autonomous beings within psychic space. This tradition goes back thousands of years. Homer (~750 BC), at the very beginning of *The Odyssey*, first calls on his Muse:

*Sing in me, Muse, and through me tell the story
of that man skilled in all ways of contending...*

Granted this is performance, and Homer wasn't generating new story material, but he still had to enter his own psychic space to recover his story. And then two stanzas later, he sings:

*Of these adventures, Muse, daughter of Zeus,
tell us in our time, lift the great song again.
Begin when all the rest...*

This is more than an artifact of culture and is, in fact, a ritual and a show of respect for divine beings who were part of a deeply felt and believed religion. It is Homer's Code of Conduct. Also note that Homer had done his homework. He had a game plan. In that second quote, he tells the Muse where to begin. You can't bludgeon your way through this process. My process is different from that used by Homer. And the reason it is is that

The Iris of Time

my Unconscious told me what it wanted. To ignore that request would be to start off with a bad precedent and a show of disrespect.

However, I do believe that once you have your psychic space set up and have developed a procedure, the rules of engagement, i.e., Code of Conduct, may be relaxed. This is also the place where I tell you not to be too particular about the purity of the process. It will take a while to become comfortable with Active Imagination, and I still have much to say about how to go about it. It will also take a while for you to understand what your Unconscious wants from you. So sit back, relax, and I'll give you a few pointers, and the most important problem to tackle is how to get the Active Imagination experience down on paper.

The first thing is to make sure you're in a room where you're not likely to be disturbed. You then lean back, close your eyes, and clean off a section of psychic space. But here's the problem. You can't take a camcorder in with you. You could rely on your memory of what happens and quickly type it into your word processor after the session. I've noticed that when I write at night using Active Imagination during my periods of insomnia, the next day I have little memory of what I wrote, or even if I wrote anything. I can't remember what I wrote until I read it. Since I'm doing this when close to sleep, is it any wonder that I can't remember it very well? I'm writing while mostly within the Land of Forgetting or the Land of Not Knowing. This is the Unconscious after all, and it's called that for a reason. So memory is a terrible place to store a session.

What to do?

You could use a voice recorder and talk about what you see and hear. I thought of this, but for me, the sound of my own voice was too much of a distraction. If this works for you, problem solved. You can transfer what you said to a word processor after the session using voice recognition software. If not, perhaps what I have learned is for you. Plus, if you're writing in bed and have a sleeping mate, you can do it in the dark without making a lot of noise. It's my solution, but it may be one you can use or perhaps adapt to your situation.

I have an iPhone with Apple's word processor application called Pages. I write primarily during three time periods: (1) when I first go to bed at night, (2) when I wake during the night, and (3) when I first wake in the morning. I've also successfully practiced it in the afternoon using a sleep mask. I generate this material while typing blind on a Bluetooth keyboard linked to my iPhone. An iPad would work just as well.

What I type shows up in my Pages app, which is linked to the document in iCloud. I cover the iPhone with a book to maintain complete darkness. I edit the material the next day. My Active Imagination sessions are all conducted within the Philosopher's Stone, which I enter and exit using my Code of Conduct.

Figure 8-3 Setup for Recording Active Imagination

The good thing about the iPhone is that it wakes up anytime I press a key on the keyboard. It then goes back to sleep when I stop typing. This is also true of the iPad. (This iPhone and iPad behavior may change with future iOS updates.) Granted, typing

The Iris of Time

while involved in Active Imagination is a distraction, and a big one at first. However, after doing this for a couple of weeks, I became oblivious to it. You keep your fingers positioned by feeling the little bumps on the "f" and "j" keys. I put a small piece of tape on the "return" key. The trick is not to care about typos or any other mistakes and just proceed. Editing takes time, but the quality of the material that comes from the process is worth the clean up effort.

Another good thing about typing it out real time is that it demands that you focus on each event of the entry process. This keeps you awake. If you're doing this just before sleep, you'll frequently drop off into dreamland without accomplishing anything. Typing keeps a portion of the intellect active and enables you to get even closer to the dream state without actually entering. Also, the mind is a quick, nimble entity and wishes to get on with it by zipping through the ritual. Typing out your actions slows the process and allows transitional effects within the psyche to take place. Concentrate on the process and notice the psychic changes you are going through. Don't remain remote from the process but become emotionally engaged. Ritual may seem mundane, but it is the heart and soul of transitioning to a new psychic state. Don't sell it short.

We are all aware of some of the processes that go on inside the mind all the time. The most universal is what we know as internal dialogue, what we think, and this mostly comes from the ego. The other process is what we know as "the mind's eye." It's practically impossible to have a thought, which we normally think of as words, without an accompanying visual stream. When someone describes a person, house or even a tree, a mental picture immediately comes to mind and matures as you describe it. This is the imagination responding to stimuli. Our task is to jump-start the imagination, and then let it go on its own.

The imagination is an ordered but autonomous-functioning part of the Unconscious that steps forward when Consciousness confronts it. Consciousness must be accepting of the Unconscious, or it will not participate at all. The Unconscious is at first incredibly shy and unassuming in the presence of Consciousness, but it may become aggressive, arrogant and intolerant if given leeway. The problem is that the Unconscious does all the hard work, and Consciousness gets all the credit. However, it also may be accepting and tolerant. It just depends on the entity that has stepped forward. Consciousness must be accepting and yet suspicious of this activity within the Unconscious because evil lurks there as well. Consciousness must always be on its guard. Some evil must be dealt with and exploited because it plays a part in the world we depict in our fiction.

I've found that going into Active Imagination without a definite purpose doesn't work. At times, I will see images and hear voices, but the encounters don't go anywhere. Having a definite purpose, as Jung suggests, directly related to what I'm writing enables me to encounter specific psychic entities, view their activities and/or engage them in dialogue. I realize that this may seem a little overly dramatic, but it is a process that has developed naturally for me, and the seeming artificiality of it may be just another manifestation of Consciousness attempting to invalidate the processes of the Unconscious. The ego ever seems to be the enemy of the process as well as always trying to invalidate information from the Unconscious. My experience with Active Imagination has been that proper preparation is crucial for success.

How can I be sure you will see images? Of course, the answer is that I can't. However, realize that the Unconscious is always active. Here's what Jung has to say about it:

> *We are quite probably dreaming all the time, but consciousness makes so much noise that we no longer hear the dream when awake.* [*Children's Dreams*, page 3]

The trick then, it would seem, is to quieten Consciousness, direct internal dialogue toward storytelling, and engage for that deeper level of the psyche, the Unconscious, to take over the narrative.

★

The Iris of Time

Okay. We've been there, done that, and now we're ready to terminate the Active Imagination session. We just open our eyes and walk away. Right?

Not so fast.

When you go into something with a ritual, you also have to be respectful of how you get out. This is the other half of the Code of Conduct. Going into the Iris of Time properly was crucial, and coming back out is also pivotal, for a couple of reasons. First of all, the exit ritual brings you back out of the liminal experience and allows you to be fully within reality. It terminates the process.

It also seems that since the Iris of Time experience is confronting the Unconscious head on, for those who might have difficulty with the Unconscious wishing to flood Consciousness with content, developing a process to turn it off is reasonable and possibly necessary. It could very well help promote better mental health in the face of a powerful but unwieldy creative tool.

Again, take your time when coming back through the Iris of Time. Keep typing. Reverse the entry process, and thank the psychic entities that help you come back out. Even a nod will do. They are now your psychic coworkers, even probably your psychic family. I know that this seems unnecessary, but it's not the act so much as it is the proper configuration of Consciousness relative to the Unconscious that's important. Tidiness leads to good mental health. It also builds respect for your own precious psychic processes. If you've imagined going in, you should imagine coming out and experience it as fully as possible, otherwise you're not being serious about it.

I've found that once I've made contact with psychic entities, sometimes they don't want to stop talking, and words and images continue to flood through the Iris even though I thought I had closed it. I suppose this is proof that you've built a bridge across the chasm, and you're using it. So this is not necessarily a bad thing, particularly if you have closed it and started editing the material. Having a close connection with the Unconscious while editing makes for a very creative session.

Story Alchemy

I realize that all this talk about psychic beings as if they are neighbors down the street sounds too literal and strange. It's just that this metaphorical way of dealing with the Unconscious is the only one available. It's like dealing with a computer as if it has a desktop, folders, files, and applications, when a computer really only contains zeroes and ones. Even that is one step from actuality because computer memory only has "on" and "off" states. We need the desktop metaphor to communicate with it, to convert its methodology and language into something with which humans can relate. Complex processes within the Unconscious dictate elaborate metaphors for Consciousness to understand. It's the way we do business together.

I suppose it all boils down to the fact that Consciousness becomes lost in the Land of Story. It needs help finding its way everywhere it goes. You'll become more familiar and confident in that land if you develop the tools and skills to negotiate it. You can use what I've learned as a dropping off point, but as time goes by, you'll be able to develop your own methods. Perhaps your Unconscious will show you the way as mine did me.

Now that you've finally passed through the Iris, it's time to check out Storyland.

CHAPTER 9 The Land of Story

The first time you step through the Iris of Time, you feel a cool breath of fresh air against your cheek, hear the soft chuckles of children, and before you, you're confronted with the inside of your dodecahedron. Each pentagon is a sheet of fine cut diamond. Each apex sparkles like a new star. You see the thin trace of each line that forms the intersections of the plot pentagons, but you can see through the flat diamond surfaces to the divine sphere that glows a faint blue with deep darkness beyond. You see the whirl of fire-breathing dragons that circumnavigate each pentagon.

The scene shifts, and you realize that you are standing on a thin, slightly arched adamantine bridge, Jung's Transcendent Function, which extends out into the center of the dodecahedron, where a woman in soft-flowing silk sits on a tripod, with nine beautiful girls in a circle about her, the source of the chuckles. The woman looks for all the world like a priestess. (I recognize her as the woman who left the key in the cupboard for me to open the mechanism that very first time.)

You advance along the bridge, and the laughter stops realizing you've come among them. The woman takes her eyes from the girls, turns to look at you and smiles like a goddess. Of course, she is. This is Mnemosyne, Goddess of Memory, and her nine daughters, the Muses. You've prepared a gift for them, and now you hand it to the mother, she accepts it and slowly undoes the twine holding the wrapper, which unfolds when she pulls the string. Inside is a golden box in the shape of a pentagon, and when she lifts the lid, she sees ten sparkling pieces of bright colored candy. Each selects a piece, puts it to her lips and touches it with the tip of her tongue.

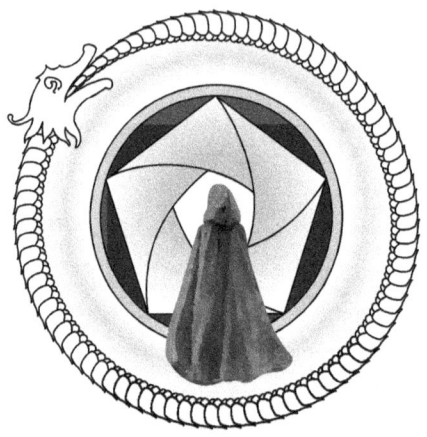

Figure 9-1 Entering the Iris of Time

The dodecahedron, bridge, and the goddesses dissolve into the framework of your universe, your creation. You are in the land of your story, and it slowly appears about you, emerging from the mists of divine memory. You hear the song of the Muses, a chorus that transforms into accompaniment for the voice of your narrator, and the words of your story come to you as the scene you are creating precipitates out of the sands of time, your characters already in motion, and you realize that yours is not an act of creation at all but one of discovery. It'd been there in psychic space all along.

This is the craft of the storyteller who possesses the Philosopher's Stone.

★

Now that we're inside, what are we doing here? Well, we should have prepared ourselves before hand. And of course, we did. That's

The Land of Story

the reason we knew how to position the Ouroboros to stimulate the appropriate portion of the plot pentagon. You did remember to do that, didn't you? That positioning prepared psychic space for us to enter at the designated location and point in time in the story. It's a step in your Code of conduct. Everyone should have a guide, a facilitator, in psychic space, and this is where we come to our first encounter with an autonomous psychic entity, other than the goddesses, of course, who are, well, goddesses. Who would you suppose it to be? Who would be sitting at the center, the dodecahedron bindu, when the mother and daughters are no longer there? That's right, the narrator of your story. She/he is the one you will channel.

So this is our first task: contacting the narrator; i.e., contacting a voice to tell the story. The first time you go inside, it can be a little frightening. What if no one steps forward to narrate your story? What if no psychic entities appear to play the parts? Well, here's the thing. If you've ever written a story before, you've done this. It's just become a much more conscious act, and a little intimidating because we've turned a spotlight on the process, and it's not fond of bright lights. You must remember that this is the dark subterranean world of the Unconscious. You wonder if this is a good idea. It's become so complicated, and the process so literally exposed that you'll never get it to work. Where's that window? You may want to jump.

Whoa! Come back inside off that ledge. Here's help.

When you first contemplated your story and came up with the idea, you essentially did contact your narrator. You met her/him/it again when you visualized your initial idea and got it to animate. You even found conflict between characters. These are all familiar processes and a part of Active Imagination, but also you could hear the words as these images flowed through your mind. This is what happens in the plot dodecahedron, the Imaginarium of the alchemist-cum-storyteller.

Let's stop for a minute and realize that we've found a new name for this thing we've been calling the Philosopher's Stone.

Story Alchemy

Since this is a tool specifically for the author, the teller of tales, we need a new name, one that suggests all the power of the Stone but with the added restriction that it's just for storytelling. More specifically, it's the birthplace for stories, the womb where the story is conceived and experiences its gestation period before it comes out into the world. This is the Imaginarium.

How do we imagine this story into existence? To imagine is simply to call the Unconscious into action. The activation of the imagination is simply a request sent to the Unconscious. If I ask you to think of a giraffe, immediately an image comes to mind, an animal with an extraordinarily long neck and forelegs. I would be willing to bet that you even envisioned its surroundings. Possibly you saw her in the wilds of Africa with a small but tall calf eating tender leaves from the top of a tree. Even if you hadn't, upon reading my words, you did then see an image. You couldn't stop yourself.

Activating the imagination is much like that, an interrogation. The process of imagining is a dialogue between Consciousness and the Unconscious. I'd be willing to bet that you had an image when I first mentioned contacting your narrator. You had to. As Aristotle put it, "Without an image thinking is impossible." [*On Memory*, Ref 450a1] You can't think about the personification of a narrator without an image coming to mind. Your job is to capture that image and expand upon it.

And images don't exclusively come from memory either. Some, perhaps even most, are fresh and come from the imagination. As you might expect, memory and imagination are connected:

> *Accordingly, if asked, of which among the parts of the soul memory is a function, we reply: manifestly of that part to which imagination also appertains; and all objects of which there is imagination are in themselves objects of memory, while those which do not exist without imagination are objects of memory incidentally.* [Aristotle, *On Memory*, 450a21-25].

This is the same as saying that Mnemosyne is the mother of the Muses who bring inspiration. Memory is the mother of the

The Land of Story

imagination. Memory is a storage container that permits retrieval. The more we put into memory, the more imagination we have. The two aren't equivalent, but they are connected and work synergistically. The imagination doesn't just have to rely on what you have previously seen. Remember that the archetypes of the Collective Unconscious are images. Later on, we'll devote a full chapter to this relationship between memory and imagination. Just realize that having a need for something activates the imagination. It's the nature of the process.

This is easy stuff, but what makes it seem difficult is that we think we have to do something "special" to get the creative juices flowing. Well, you do. And that "special" thing is to realize that you've already done it. Your imagination is always way ahead of you. Way ahead. Your problem is to catch up. These images are so pale, and we're so used to not acknowledging them that we have difficulty believing they are that important. In getting a glimpse of one, you've caught your imagination at work, and when you step inside the Imaginarium, your imagination should blossom because that's where you'll find all the secrets concerning your story.

We have an offshoot of Jungian psychology that just might be of assistance in understanding how natural and powerful this process is. It's called archetypal psychology. Archetypal psychology is "deliberately affiliated with the arts, culture, and the history of ideas, arising as they do from the imagination." [Hillman, *Archetypal Psychology*, page 1] James Hillman, who founded archetypal psychology, tells us, "archetypes are the primary forms that govern the psyche." He goes on to say that:

> *The primary, and irreducible, language of these archetypal patterns is the metaphorical discourse of myths. These can therefore be understood as the most fundamental patterns of human existence.* [page 3]

This means that the soul is a storytelling mechanism. And then comes the clincher:

> *The archetypal images are the fundamentals of fantasy, they are the*

means by which the world is imagined, and therefore they are the modes by which all knowledge, all experiences whatsoever become possible. [page 12]

He also says, "the archetype is accessible to imagination first and first presents itself as image." [page 4] What this means is that the intricate thought processes of the mind originate in images, and you can't keep your mind from producing them. Our task is to catch our minds performing their most basic function. Once we realize what is going on, all we have to do is make a request, and the mind will produce images.

Your narrator can stay in the background, or you can bring him/her/it forward. Use the Iris of Time along with the Code of Conduct provides access to the Imaginarium to activate the Unconscious and provide a separate psychic space within which you can write the novel. Become involved in the process, and let the material flow to you, accepting the content but evaluating its appropriateness. In working out this appropriateness, you consult with your narrator. You have established a working relationship. Graphically, it all looks like this:

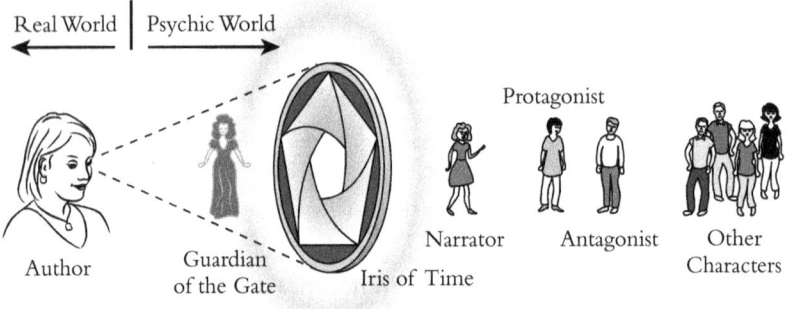

Figure 9-2 Story Alchemy - Psychic Process - The Imaginarium

The graphic shows the author with his/her Consciousness, the Iris of Time with the Guardian of the Gate standing before it, the narrator, and then the protagonist alongside the antagonist, and a crowd of people beyond them representing the rest of the characters.

The Land of Story

As you enter, muster as many of the senses as you can manage. Notice some new detail at each step, and pay attention to what you hear, feel and smell every time you go inside. Even the repetition of senses causes them to become more pronounced and deepens the experience. Touch the metallic frame of the Iris when you go through, feel the cold, slick surface. Feel the gust of air from the new environment when you step inside. Is it cool and fresh? Or possibly hot and smoky, a dystopian landscape screaming with discontent? The senses help ground you in this psychic world and make it come alive. You don't have to imagine the Muses each time you enter, but it's best to envision the narrator, make contact and request her/him/it provide whatever services you require. From here on, the process is the same as it ever was. You write your story. But now it should come alive as never before. You should be able to visualize it in 3D and with full Technicolor.

★

By stepping into the Imaginarium, the author has entered the liminal state within which she/he will not just "make up" the story but actually experience it. But the author must not stay remote from its emotional impact. Jung says:

> ...*if you recognize your own involvement you yourself must enter into the process with your personal reactions, just as if you were one of the fantasy figures, or rather, as if the drama being enacted before your eyes were real. It is a psychic fact that this fantasy is happening, and it is as real as you — as a psychic entity — are real.* [*Mysterium Coniunctionis*, page 529]

To induce this state fully, not only must you use the Iris of Time, but you will also have to invest yourself in the outcome of the action. Here's what James Hall has to say:

> ...*liminality requires that the ego-centrum itself disidentify from the dominant self-image, undergo the experiences associated with the liminal state, and then reidentify with a self-image that is usually more comprehensive and inclusive than the original image.* [*Liminality and Transitional Phenomena*, ed. by Nathan Schwartz-Salant and

Murray Stein; James A. Hall, "The Watcher at the Gates of Dawn," page 44]

Give yourself up, your real-world identity, and participate in the process, whether as a closely connected viewer of the action or as a participant, possibly even your protagonist for a first-person narrative. One thing I believe is true about entering so deeply into psychic space is that you keep your Consciousness but lose your identity, at least you lose your earthly identity. You are of indeterminate age and origin until you reidentify upon exiting.

All Active Imagination techniques presuppose that the author has laid a lot of groundwork to familiarize him/herself with the fictional world and characters, as well as the issues that provide meaning to the story. Every gift from the Unconscious comes wrapped in contents from Consciousness. The thing is that if no Consciousness material exists, the Unconscious will package the contents with material of its own choosing, and it then may not be recognizable as story related. That seems to be the reason that to gain inspiration, the author must go into Active Imagination having primed Consciousness. You already have images associated with your story, so you're not waiting for anything to appear. You started playing around with them back in Chapter 2 when you developed your story's premise. I can't begin to tell you how important these images and voices are to what you're about to do. Since you know what the conflict is about and have identified the protagonist and antagonist, you already have an idea as to their appearance and actions in which they are involved. That isn't to say they won't evolve. Particularly during the initial states of conceiving a story, everything will be up for grabs.

Since you've configured the Iris of Time for your story, once you step through the Iris, you are in the fictional world of that story. In other words, you're inside the story dodecahedron, the Imaginarium. Lucy has entered through the wardrobe and what lies before her is Narnia. If you are at one of your plot points or even an intermediate point, the fact that you conceived the scene means that you have mental images associated with it. The

The Land of Story

trick is to capture those images with Consciousness and let them animate. The characters within those images should start acting out your story.

If you look around, you should be able to envision what this fictional world looks like. It isn't ordinary reality. Look for the aspects of that fictional world that make it unique. A good example might be a movie from a few years back, *Sky Captain and the World of Tomorrow* since it has an otherworldly look. Yours shouldn't necessarily look like that; it's just that it does look like an altered reality and illustrates that this fictional world has to be characterized to fit the story. In a way, all stories are paintings — some watercolors, some oils, others ink sketches. And you must apply the craft to bring that fictional/mythic world to life.

I know you'll undoubtedly say that you've set your story in the real world, so no shift is necessary, but that's just not true. I'm not telling you to make it look different. I'm telling you that it will be different. It's a characteristic of Storyland. Setting is one of the most effective tools an author has, and characterizing that fictional world is a big part of the story. It's a characterized reality. That's quite probably the first lesson we learn when we enter the Imaginarium. Everything within this fictional world is slanted to accommodate the story. In movies, they frequently use digital grading to shift real-world images into the Land of Story. This doesn't mean that it has to look like Faery Land. It's a unique world and should look special. So make sure you look around and see what makes it surreal, as all fictional worlds are. All stories have a mythical quality and even if your story is set in the real world, it has a mythical counterpart of which you should be aware and describe to your readers. In the Imaginarium, you need to be your own cinematographer, set designer, and digital editor. Everything your reader encounters must be story specific. The world in which it is set is no exception.

Be patient. Active Imagination techniques develop and perfect over time, and since it is at once both a specific process and in many ways an unimaginable one, you must experience it for yourself to learn to work with it. I have identified seven levels of Active Imagination. Four through seven are advanced levels that involve the dream state, and I've relegated them to the next chapter. All levels occur within the Imaginarium.

Level One: Normal Writing. Level One is undoubtedly what you already do with your normal writing process. You sit at your computer and type while imagining your story. This process has worked well throughout the ages, although it's not been recognized as related to Jung's Active Imagination. It is a hybrid process where the author is unaware of the connection with her/his Unconscious, yet she/he has direct access to her/his characters. You may use the Iris of Time, but it is optional. The author may then augment this with what Burroway calls "freewriting" and "clustering" [*Writing Fiction*, 4-12] to let the Unconscious have a more direct say.

Level Two: Active Imagination. This is the first step in adapting Jung's Active Imagination to writing fiction. It's a deeper psychic state that pulls more heavily on content from the Unconscious, and it's what I envision as happening within the Iris of Time and involves the full Code of Conduct. This is also a daytime process, but while using it, you have your eyes closed, perhaps using a sleeping mask, and although you may be typing at the moment, you focus on that space within your psyche, which you have cleared to allow Active Imagination. Early afternoon, siesta time, is perfect for this. You might write before your nap and again immediately afterward. You seek out settings within your novel, explore roads, buildings, but also encounter psychic entities to observe and/or actively engage in conversation. These entities are your narrator and characters. Your story unfolds in real time, and you type it out as it occurs. Once the session is complete, you take that material and adapt it to your work in progress.

Level Three: Twilight Zone. This level of Active Imagination occurs at night, either just before sleep, upon waking in the middle of the night, or just after waking in the morning. It also occurs within the Imaginarium as entered through the

The Land of Story

Iris of Time with the full Code of Conduct. You can record your activity as it happens on a notebook computer or afterward if your memory serves you well. What is good about this method is that you're already in a liminal state because you are close to sleep. This is my favorite writing technique.

In the next chapter we'll discuss the other four methods.

★

Just as with the yantra and the mandala, the Imaginarium has two modes. In mandala mode, or "narrating mode," we see the setting and characters at each plot point, the story unfolds, and we hear the words of the narrator residing at the bindu. The second, or yantra mode, is what I call "plotting mode." We view it as an entirely geometric object: a bindu, pentagram, pentagon and the assembled dodecahedron, all enclosed within a sphere.

When involved in plotting the story and making connections, the intellect is more involved than when writing dramatic material. You are in a psychic position more emotionally removed from the action and experience a different creative state. You see the beauty of the overall structure and the intricacy of connections as you watch the events fall into place like the pieces of a jigsaw puzzle. We tend to think of the intellect as being unemotional, but the impact on the author when this intricate story structure starts to come together can be quite profound.

★

When you, through Active Imagination, bring content from your Unconscious into the real world, that content is not ready for the story. It still must undergo a transformation to be fully compatible with that specific fictional world. The narrator makes this transformation, i.e., the author transforms the content by use of narrative craft. Graphically this editing process as the story gains definition and brilliance goes through stages something like Figure 9-3. When you start editing this content once outside the Active Imagination session, it provides a subliminal bridge to the Unconscious and permits additional high-quality content to cross over. The process feeds on itself. You've generated the story material inside the far reaches of the psyche, and while editing, it takes you back there but less consciously.

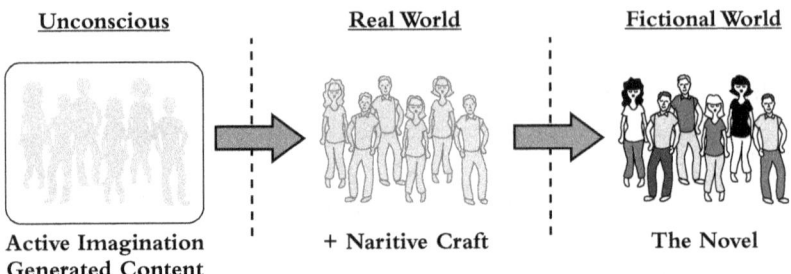

Figure 9-3 Editing

According to my way of thinking, the narrator guides you in the world of the Unconscious, works with you, and helps transform the content into narration. But you still have to do the legwork. You will have to transform the content to achieve the narrative stance and voice consistent with the novel. You might think that the narrator is not doing her/his/its job, but the narrator is your guide and advisor in creating the narrative flow. She/he/it supplies the voice, but you, as the author, are always the one who does the legwork.

One of the first things you'll notice is that not all dialogue from the Unconscious sounds realistic. Here's what Jung has to say about dialogue with psychic beings from the Collective Unconscious, i.e., archetypes:

First I formulated the things as I had observed them, usually in "high-flown language," for that corresponds to the style of the archetypes. Archetypes speak the language of high rhetoric, even of bombast. [Memories, Dreams, Reflections, pages 177/8]

Although it may have its uses, this certainly will not go over well for most storytelling. As a matter of fact, this might go a long way toward explaining why dialogue so frequently goes astray. It comes to us unadorned, so to speak, without the idiomatic touches that characterize the way we converse in the real world.

I realize that this editing process seems laborious, uninteresting,

The Land of Story

and simple-minded cleanup work. You couldn't be more wrong. This is possibly the most important stage of writing. Your Consciousness slipped across the boundary that we call the Iris of Time, and confronted the Unconscious head-on. You spent a good amount of time there. Now Consciousness must work on that material on its own turf. It must spend even more time perfecting it than did the Unconscious in generating it. This is where ego consciousness gets the upperhand.

Editing is the final step in the process that forms the bridge between Consciousness and the Unconscious, the Transcendent Function. In many ways, this constitutes meditation on the mandala. Jung spent decades rewriting his Active Imagination sessions, and he documented them in *The Red Book*. The Transcendent Function is something that we work on our entire lives, but we get something from using Active Imagination for creating a story, and that is the work itself. The story is the real-world representation of the Transcendent Function. It's not all of it but does represent the labor done on the Transcendent Function during that time period. It cannot be perfected without a lot of hard work by Consciousness. This is where we turn lead into gold.

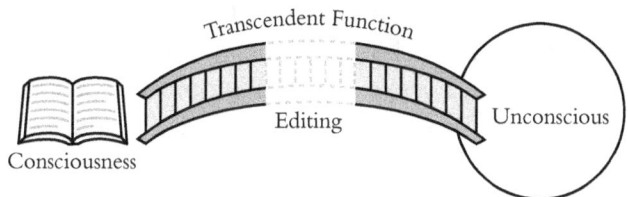

Figure 9-4 Editing Effects on the Transcendent Function

When editing becomes difficult, it's because the bridge between this material and its location in the Unconscious is still tentative. That part of the Transcendent Function is still under construction. Perhaps both sides of the bridge aren't quite connected. Another possibility is that Consciousness and the Unconscious are still negotiating the material. The competing factions can't come to terms with how it should be presented without the editing process.

Story Alchemy

You should understand that the editing process is much more than just clean up work. It's a continuation and completion of the creative act and is very much involved in Consciousness/Unconscious conflict that leads toward resolution. This perception adds an element of intrigue that helps relish getting involved in it. Other approaches to editing make it sound like dog work that has little intrinsic value. Just realize that it is a deeply spiritual process that completes the personal (psychic) and artistic (gold) transmutation.

Failure. What do you do when the process just doesn't work? I have experienced this although I must say that Active Imagination is remarkably easy and repeatable. But if it doesn't work, it's disappointing. That is until you realize that failure, even in these situations, rarely has occurred. I'm not just trying to bolster your spirits. I have learned that in the hours and days following a "failed" Active Imagination session, the work I wished to accomplish actually had been. It just hadn't as yet come into Consciousness. If it was a problem, it's been solved. If I was trying to develop a scene, it came to me the next day.

Whatever the case, you shouldn't assume that you've failed. Sometimes the old expression, "I need to sleep on it," works best. Don't get discouraged. Nothing disrupts the creative process like disillusionment. Except that disillusionment is also a part of the process, but that's another story, and one I'll address in just a moment.

★

At the risk of getting overly repetitious, I want to reiterate something I've already gone over. It has to do with the nature of the psychic world and in particular the reality of that world. The Land of Story I've called it. This is possibly the biggest stumbling block for students of authorial craft to digest, or even possibly take seriously. The entities you meet there are autonomous and as real in psychic space as you are in the real world. Yet, your first inclination is to invalidate everything you find there. We speak of it as being "fictional." This is Consciousnes's first line of defense.

The Land of Story

The proof that the entities we meet in the psychic world are autonomous and real exists in our dreams. All of us have encountered people that we have never met in real life, and these people have autonomy and speak their own minds. We have no evidence that they are anything but spirits of another world. This leads me to say that you should not only give your characters autonomy, but also recognize their own inherent autonomy. The fictional character you have "invented" already has its autonomy, but the intellect is just not used to seeing it that way. This can be difficult because it means that the problem is one of reinterpreting a process that already exists and not one of developing a new skill.

Realizing that you must obey a Code of Conduct to deal with these psychic entities reinforces what Jung said about dealing with them: to always treat them with respect even if you don't agree with what they say or do. When you address your narrator within the psychic world, you further divorce your own ego from those psychic entities. They are "out there." Other. Not you. This allows them more autonomy, and your conversations with your narrator prepare you for the observation of the other psychic entities. This technique of getting into the Active Imagination state sets up and prepares your psyche so that you'll have a good chance of accomplishing your objective.

To more fully understand the writing process using Jung's Active Imagination, I suggest visualizing it as a relationship most of us have experienced. It's a big-sibling/little-sibling concept, as shown in Figure 9-5, with the older (Consciousness) scolding and browbeating the younger (the Subconscious). This represents both Consciousness and the Unconscious residing in the author, with Consciousness always invalidating material from the Unconscious. The irony is that the Unconscious, which is in fact much larger and much older than Consciousness, simply occupies a submissive position so that it must surreptitiously provide its influence. The Unconscious never gets to attend the awards ceremony.

Authors are famous for becoming disillusioned with their work. It is possible that Consciousness's skill at keeping material at bay through denial and invalidation now becomes a major force in evaluating its worth. It seems that everything that is force-fed into Consciousness comes with an element of invalidation, and the more material that crosses the bridge, the more disillusioned Consciousness will be with it. The author has developed an aversion to her/his own work.

Figure 9-5 Contentious Little-Brother/Big-Brother Relationship between the Unconscious and Consciousness

For Active Imagination to work, you must have faith (confidence) in the material coming from the Unconscious. Thus, through time, we come to trust Active Imagination and take what we uncover practicing it seriously. When we do that, the Unconscious gains confidence and provides more important and well thought out material. But also Consciousness's interpretation of the material is put on firmer ground, and we gain insight into it. If we don't have faith, we gain nothing and learn nothing. It becomes trivial because the material that comes across is trivial, and Consciousness invalidates it.

If all this talk about faith starts to sound a little like religion, that is because it is precisely what religious people talk about. Once you start questioning the process, it breaks down. You must have faith to get the process to work. But faith has a down side. Faith has lead directly to disillusionment. And the big thing here is to realize that this disillusionment is a part of the process.

Once material from the Unconscious is brought into Consciousness and Consciousness takes an objective look at it, the apparent worth of the material starts to break down because Consciousness always has a derogatory opinion of everything that comes from the Unconscious. That's the way it protects itself from being flooded by it. All this is a part of what we know as the Transcendent Function.

Faith and disillusionment seem to be flip sides of the same coin. Perhaps even more concretely, they are like matter and antimatter. When they come together, they annihilate each other and then we are indifferent. This is reminiscent of Samuel Coleridge's famous statement that, when he was embarking on a particularly imaginative writing project:

...*my endeavours should be directed to persons and characters supernatural, or at least romantic, yet so as to transfer from our inward nature a human interest and a semblance of truth sufficient to procure for these shadows of imagination that willing suspension of disbelief for the moment, which constitutes poetic faith.*

Conceivably, Coleridge's Collective Unconscious provided this mechanism to him, so that he could have a more productive creative imagination. In other words for Coleridge the Unconscious made a bargain with Consciousness. This is what enabled him to write *The Rhyme of the Ancient Mariner*. Note also that Coleridge equates "faith" with the "willing suspension of disbelief," which must be in force for Active Imagination to be productive. The practitioner of Active Imagination (while engaging psychic entities) is very much in the same position as the reader of an imaginative literary work, and the suspension of disbelief is a necessary part of the process.

All creative individuals become disillusioned with their work. Religious people also become disillusioned. Later in life, Billy Graham spoke of his own disillusionment, how he had suffered from it from time to time. I'm reminded of Christ on the cross saying, "My God, my God, why have you forsaken me?" [Matthew 27:46] Christ's own faith in his mission failed him. He had lost contact with the myth that was living him. I don't mean "myth" as something not true, but "myth" as the highest form of wisdom and enlightenment.

Of course, the opposite is also true. Once you're far enough inside, you get an archetypical dose of delusions of grandeur and believe what you're writing is the greatest thing ever put on paper. This isn't such a bad deal, because delusion facilitates the process of creation. However, it does taint it with an overestimation of the worth of the work that might not go away after returning from the creative recesses. Storytelling is an adult task that takes a steady hand at the wheel to reel in both overly positive and negative feelings about your work.

★

After having visited the psychic space inside the Imaginarium, let's now take it all a step deeper. Planning ahead and learning to negotiate that liminal space just before sleep can yield some startling results. Let's see just how far we can push the boundaries, even to the point of taking story elements inside the World of Dreams. The situations and characters you write about will at times be scary, so this may not be the most comfortable technique you've ever considered. What if you write horror stories? Others have negotiated the landscape using lucid dreaming, and we will build on their research.

Buckle up. This could be another blue-pill, red-pill moment.

CHAPTER 10 Dream Invasion

If you've been writing for a while and ever have been deeply involved in a story, you've encountered at least one of your characters in a dream. You may have even run across an antagonist or two, something that can be disconcerting and might have resulted in a nightmare. In short, you've suffered a dream invasion.

By "dream invasion" I mean both dreams invading your story, and your story invading your dreams. Both will happen automatically. I dreamed about my protagonist when I wrote *The Escape of Bobby Ray Hammer*, so much so that the memory of his fictional life in my own hometown became in many ways more powerful than the memory of my own. After one such dream, I became concerned he'd take over my psychic space including my memories. The exercise for the author is to accentuate the intuitive activity and assume a measure of control.

Let's take a minute to see how creative writing might affect your dreams. First of all, you have a dream life that was well established before you started writing. Second, some of your dreams will have perturbations caused by this new story. Third, you'll have dream perturbations caused by "becoming worthy." Remember my dream of finding my own body lying in a gutter? Fourth, you'll have dream perturbations related to your craft. An example of this is the dream I had concerning what I initially thought was a large bank vault but that I came to associate with the plot mandala/yantra, which became the Iris of Time.

It's important to pay attention to your initial dream state and watch for changes caused by Active Imagination and other aspects of creative writing. I suggest documenting your more-important dreams. This will help you understand what is going on in your own psychic space. People change over time, and using Active Imagination for creative storytelling may very well accelerate the change.

Since creative writing affects dreams, we need to learn more about the process and how we might harness it. First, we should look at how Jung thought of dreams. Here are summaries of what Jung saw as four possible origins [*Children's Dreams*, page 4/5]:

1. The dream is the unconscious reaction to a conscious situation.
2. The dream depicts a situation that originated in a conflict between consciousness and the unconscious.
3. The dream represents that tendency of the unconscious that aims at a change of the conscious attitude.
4. The dream depicts unconscious processes showing no relation to the conscious situation. ...They are like an oracle...

The first three definitions deal directly with the relationship between Consciousness and the Unconscious and should be helpful. The fourth might be pertinent on some level, but we'll set it aside for now.

The first might be useful because the author has setup a situation, albeit what he/she believes to be an artificial one in the form of a story, about which the Unconscious may wish to react. I prefer to look at this as a reasoned dream response rather than a mechanical necessity or a knee-jerk reaction from the Unconscious. Freewill exists in the Unconscious just as it does within Consciousness. An example of this would be when an author has an idea for a story but can't quite visualize its overall arc. The Unconscious would provide a dream to reveal more of

Dream Invasion

the plotline but perhaps dressed in different clothing.

The second definition involves an internal conflict that already exists, and as such, naturally feeds into our concept of story. If our story originated subconsciously from a conflict between Consciousness and the Unconscious, we're really in luck because both are already engaged in this storytelling. We only have to get that existing conflict into the World of Dreams. This in all likelihood has already occurred but with a different adaptation that would obscure its origin.

The third definition borders on being conflict but is perhaps a precursor where the Unconscious first identifies something in Consciousness, makes a comment, and waits for a reaction. If Consciousness accepts the comment, we never experience conflict, and if so, it doesn't provide help with our story. If Consciousness rejects the comment, the Unconscious may just walk away and nothing results, but if it refuses to give it up, then we have a conflict, and it reverts to the second definition.

It would seem then that definition two would be most beneficial. After all, the central conflict came from the Unconscious. If we take a conflict into a dream, something that has already resonated with Consciousness, we may be able to investigate it further in the World of Dreams. We've all had nightmares, so we're definitely in the right place.

That said, one thing more. Dream invasion techniques are a work in progress, much more so than the rest of this book. I have done a certain amount of research involving dreams, enough to realize how difficult some of these techniques are and that it's undoubtedly a huge subject of which I'll never learn the full extent. But it does yield dividends. Experiment with the techniques I present in this chapter, which will include lucid dreaming. We have all experienced lucid dreaming, which is simply realizing that you're dreaming while dreaming. It would seem a natural fit.

I also want to reinforce the role my dreams and other "psychic events" played in the development of the Iris of Time, the Imaginarium, and the vampire novel I wrote during that same time period. I had dreams of a large circular mechanism in the wall of a home. I had a dream of a dragon. I had another dream of a dead body that turned out to be my own. I have had other dreams that also influenced but didn't make it into this narrative, and still more yet that related to my vampire novel, and possibly a multitude that were pertinent but upon waking I didn't remember at all.

Even though you'll have my suggestions to help guide you through the initial stages of developing your own techniques, in many ways you'll be hacking your own path into the wilderness. You should seriously consider keeping track of your learning process because it will be of benefit later on. Your process will mature, and if you don't keep track of it, you'll forget what you learned early on. You're in this for the long haul, and that means years, so keep circling back to review what you learned earlier, something like that Ouroboros eating its own tail. Documenting it helps remember what you've learned and to trust your process. You are doing the legwork and might consider putting it out there for the benefit of the rest of the storytelling community. Creating a blog, as I did with the Iris of Time, will help for a sense of community and foster group development. We can all use the help.

So how do we go about using material from dreams when creating a story narrative? First of all, don't force yourself to interpret a dream so that it fits what you're writing. If the dream was impressive, keep it in mind, and it just might find the proper place later on. Try it on for size. If it fits, use it. If it's a stretch, don't. It's that simple, and that complex. We don't always immediately understand our internal processes and what the Unconscious is trying to tell us. It can take time, sometimes years.

Let's return now to our discussion of the methods of using Active Imagination that we suspended in the previous chapter. We have four states left to discuss. Here, we dive deep into the dream process.

Level Four: Event Horizon. This level of Active

Dream Invasion

Imagination occurs when you clear psychic space and enter the Iris of Time to create a visual and auditory state at the very edge of sleep. You are at the Event Horizon of the Black Hole. You always go into the state with a purpose, but still leave yourself open to whatever comes, within reason. You will see vivid images. These are essentially dream images, and you are very close to the dream state, but with practice, you can achieve a certain stability at the edge of the abyss. In time, you can learn to prolong this state until it becomes an extremely productive session.

You cannot actively record what is happening because it will pull you out of the state. You will either have to rely on your memory or, after experiencing the images and voices, you will have to interrupt the session to record it, essentially dropping back to the keyboard state (Level Three) of Active Imagination. Then you will record the images and voices and be actively adding to the experience because Active Imagination expands upon memory in the retelling. The more you try to remember, the more you are adding to and perhaps even changing what happened. This state may also be used casually to familiarize yourself with the setting of your novel. You can enter the fictional world, walk around, talk to people related and unrelated to your story and visit locations that you will never use as a setting.

Level Five: Entering the Black Hole. This level of Active Imagination occurs when you again clear away psychic space, enter the Iris of Time, and try to maintain your presence there as you fall asleep. Initially, you are at the Event Horizon of the Black Hole, but this time you allow yourself to slip inside. You always go into the state with a purpose, but instead of leaving yourself open to whatever comes, you try to define the world you enter and possibly drag one or more of your characters with you.

Practice this level anytime just before sleep. In this technique, you actively take your story, or an element of it, into the dream state with you. You can engage one or more of your characters using Active Imagination and then have them accompany you into your dream, constantly engaging them in conversation while allowing sleep to overtake you. This is an attempt to profoundly affect the nature of the dream. It may take on many forms.

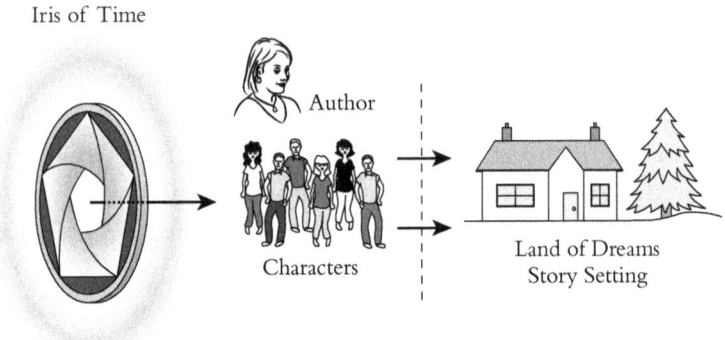

Figure 10-1 Dream Invasion

Level Six: Lucid Dreaming. In this state, you are in the middle of an existing dream when you realize that you are dreaming. If you've prepared properly, you can then remember that you wanted to accomplish something concerning your story, and you locate and actively engage characters. This can take some practice, but a guide exists to help with this sort of activity. Stephen LaBerge, a Stanford University dream researcher, wrote two books on lucid dreaming. They are: *Lucid Dreaming, the Power of Being Awake & Aware in Your Dreams*, and *Exploring the World of Lucid Dreaming* (with Howard Rheingold). They should be immensely helpful.

Level Seven: Reentry. Returning to the dream state upon waking. Again, you must do your homework beforehand. When coming out of the dream state after a long sleep, you can try to transition the dream into one related to the story, adapting the material of the dream as a template to learn more about your story. You should try to remember to reenter as soon upon waking as possible. You gather your story resources and reenter the dream world through the Iris of Time but trying to slant the dream to the world of your story. You might wish to take your characters

Dream Invasion

with you for a predetermined activity.

Once you've been inside the dream for a while, you may wish to transition to the Event Horizon and continue the session. Once you have obtained some content, you can pick up your notebook/keyboard and drop back to level three, typing out what you remember and augmenting it with whatever your imagination provides to supplement your memory.

After I had been using this technique for a few weeks, I noticed that I could relive both my dreams and Active Imagination sessions. This was more than just mulling the experience over in my mind. I relived the experience, such as it was. It's as if time does not exist within the Iris of Time. Time exists on this side of the Iris, but on the other, a primordial landscape rules, and events within it, are still there, still exist, and I only have to step again into the event to relive it. In doing so, I can retrieve more of the experience. I realize other aspects that I didn't notice the first time I lived it. The point I'm trying to get across is that I wasn't remembering the first experience. I was living the experience again, only in succeeding times I was more fully alive and in the moment. To me, this indicated that my Consciousness was more firmly imbedded in the Collective Unconscious.

The other thing that seems to be true is that time only exists in the Collective Unconscious relative to a narrative. The flow of time does not exist unless it is within a story. It's as if each story has a location within psychic space. Getting to these locations is only a matter of directing the imagination to a particular spot. Time is not involved in getting to a new location.

★

I had another dream that illustrates the connection between the author and his/her psychic drama. Initially, I had no idea what my Unconscious was trying to tell me, but a few months later, I realized that it had told how to become involved in the unfolding drama and yet retain my autonomy as well as permitting that of other psychic entities. As I came out of the dream, I transitioned to Active Imagination to keep expanding on and interpreting the ideas inherent in the dream. Here is the dream in its entirety along with my thoughts during the Active Imagination session, which I wrote down immediately afterward:

January 28, 2012, 04:30 am.

I just woke from another bizarre dream. I was in a room with five other men. Three of us were there as spectators, and the other three were actors in a play or some strange reality show. I am not sure that a large audience was viewing this. At least, they were not a part of my awareness while this was happening, although I quickly wondered about an audience soon after I woke.

The three men who were actors in this drama, and it was as close to real life as you can get, were arguing over something that had happened concerning their business that had gone wrong. One man had been in charge of some project that had gone wrong, but he was rather unconcerned about the outcome. His boss was not as flippant about it, and as far as I can remember, fired the man on the spot.

The other two members of the audience and I were sitting on a sofa in the same room with the actors, and the play was being put on for us. We could participate in the dialogue to a certain extent but could not interfere with the action. Seems that we could only comment or ask a question now and then. After his boss fired him, the man who made the mistake left the stage. And that's another thing. We were not actually on a stage. We were in a home. The entire play was being staged in a normal home that had been setup for this play.

After the man left, a woman entered, and I remember being concerned for her physical wellbeing. But it seems that they never performed that part of the play, or if they did, I've forgotten what happened. I believe it was a rape scene, and I remember being worried about the emotional impact it was going to have on me, me being in the same room with such violence toward a woman. But the next thing I remember is that the woman was gone, and another man entered. He was a large man, muscular, and in a T-shirt. He came in and sat down in an easy chair on the other side of the room from the three of us who were spectators. He started talking about two friends, or possibly business associates of his who got into a fight. He said that these were big men, and that, although they were businessmen,

Dream Invasion

they were good at fighting, really good. The implication being that both men got hurt really bad.

One of the spectators I was with asked the actor a question about what happened, and the actor interacted with him to answer the question, but then went back to scripted dialogue. The question seemed an intrusion, but that this type of questioning from the audience, the three of us, was expected and a part of how this play was presented.

I then woke, and I immediately, but impulsively, began fantasizing to extend the action of the play, envisioning the action of the fight, and the two fighters going to the hospital emergency room to get stitched up. But I also then realized what a bizarre dream I had just had, and wondered what my Collective Unconscious was trying to tell me. This dream seemed to be a take on the characteristics of visiting another family and being witnesses to their family arguments, except that this was business people, or possibly criminals, the mob or possibly drug dealers.

It is also a lot like the way I've been writing fiction. I have created my vampire novel by first creating a narrator who I go see to get her to tell me the story. I envision that I enter the Iris of Time and go see her, and we lie down together, hold hands, and she tells me the story there in the dark. We both imagine the story. I then ask her questions about her story, but we do not question our characters. Perhaps we should.

I'm reminded of Shakespeare's "Epilogue" at the end of The Tempest. This is one of the most talked about passages in all Shakespeare. Prospero talks directly to the audience and speaks as though he is both Prospero and Shakespeare. He asks the audience for its approval, by their applause of course. But it is also as if the audience has been a participant all along, sort of a god overseeing the action.

The thing I remember about the play of my dream is being both a part of the play and at the same time, not a part of the play. We were sort of a Greek chorus. We could participate in the play by asking questions and making comments, but our part in the play wasn't scripted, and we had no impact on the action. We were both in the play and outside of it. I remember that the emotional impact was quite profound. We were not in reality threatened, but we were so close to the action, and in some ways a part of it, yet not a part of it, that we could be overcome with emotion.

Story Alchemy

I thought about a Broadway play where before it began, the producers would come out on stage and select three members of the audience at random to go up on stage with the actors and experience the play from there. They could comment and ask questions, and the actors would address them, but the script would be followed to the word with these intrusions. When the play was over the three audience members who had seen the play from onstage with the actors would then debrief the audience on what the experience was like being a part, but not an actual part, of the play. The audience would be watching them watch the play.

I could also envision a large home being the stage for such a play where the audience and cast intermixed, and the members of the audience didn't know who the actors were, until of course the play began and was acted out from within the audience. The play would occur in different rooms perhaps even at the same time, and audience members that didn't see one part could explain to the others what happened at several planned breaks. Even the actors could then take part in the conversation about what had happened, as if it really had happened. Then the play would resume quite without warning, and the audience would stand around and watch the action proceed without interfering.

Of course, it would also be possible to have members of the audience become participants in the play, where an actor would request the help of a specific audience member to, say, help him kill a man. In that way, an audience member would understand or get to experience the feeling of being an actor. Perhaps, less dramatically, a member of the audience would only be asked to give the actor, say a woman, a hug. At least in some small way, at least a portion of the audience could participate in the play. I would also imagine some security people being present on the periphery to extract any members of the audience who became unruly and/or overly participatory in the action.

I can imagine this being a really powerful theatre experience. I know the limited experience in my dream was. But as with all things theatre, this has probably already been tried.

All this from a dream.

I'm sure that I even now do not fully understand this powerful and complex dream. I present it to you for your interpretation.

Dream Invasion

You, with your more objective perspective, might be able to decode more of it than I've been able to.

Participating with your characters as I did in this dream is another way to get closer to the action of the story you're telling. This is a way to practice Active Imagination around a story element. Even though it seemed to have something to do with my vampire novel, I was puzzled that night and in the days and months that followed. But when reading Jung, I realized the connection with the author's stance relative to his/her Active Imagination drama. I quoted the full passage back in Chapter 5, but it bears repeating:

What is enacted [in an Active Imagination session] *on the stage still remains a background process; it does not move the observer in any way, and the less it moves him the smaller will be the cathartic effect of this private theatre. The piece that is being played does not want merely to be watched impartially, it wants to compel his participation. If the observer understands that his own drama is being performed on this inner stage, he cannot remain indifferent to the plot and its denouement. He will notice, as the actors appear one by one and the plot thickens, that they all have some purposeful relationship to his conscious situation, that he is being addressed by the unconscious, and that it causes these fantasy-images to appear before him. He therefore feels compelled, or is encouraged by his analyst, to take part in the play and, instead of just sitting in a theatre, really have it out with his alter ego. For nothing in us ever remains quite uncontradicted, and consciousness can take up no position which will not call up, somewhere in the dark corners of the psyche, a negation or a compensatory effect, approval or resentment.* [*Mysterium Coniunctionis*, paragraph 706]

The author has to be simultaneously a member of the audience, an actor in a play, and the character. It's a divine trinity. If we envision this all happening within our story dodecahedron, it seems to satisfy all of Jung's requirements.

You will not be able to associate everything you experience in any of these dream levels with your story. The psyche has a mind of its own, and sometimes its issues and intent will supersede yours. Do not fight this or even be disappointed. After all, the conflict in your story isn't the only one your Unconscious is experiencing. The objective is to entice your Unconscious to help with your writing, not to beat it into a slave of your process. Your Unconscious is adaptable, and you should work with it, always being cognizant of its wishes, nature, and limitations. This is a partnership, one built on trust and goodwill, and you should not abuse your Unconscious with demands incompatible with its nature.

After several months of Active Imagination, I finally started making progress working with my narrator and characters. I discussed plot problems with my narrator. She helped with them. She developed into more of an autonomous person. I also learned how to work with characters in the Active Imagination context. I discussed situations with them and learned what they were experiencing. They told me their problems and how they were trying to solve them. They helped develop the story. They contended with the actual situation. I was just hearing about their problems and solutions.

While working on the third volume of *The Mysteries*, I tried to enter a dream with my characters. At the risk of boring you to death, I'll provide a little information on what I accomplished in these session. If you haven't read the first two volumes of *The Mysteries*, you'll undoubtedly be confused about the details, but you should still be able to get the gist of how my dream invasion experience worked. To help prime you for what I say below, I'll provide a link to the first six chapters of this new work: mysteriesblog.com. Here are the results of my Active Imagination:

I first entered the Iris of Time to contact my characters. I wanted to take Theonoë, one of my two protagonists, and her friend Keladeine inside with me. I also took Palaemon, a blacksmith and father to Theonoë, and his two workmen, Alkmon and Damnamenus.

I managed to be aware of their presence right after I woke early the next morning. I immediately tried to take my characters with me into a dream. I didn't actually go to sleep, and I didn't stay in one psychic

Dream Invasion

location, but I started receiving amazing flashes of my characters talking to me. I saw flashes of Eleusis in ruins, which had burned in Volume 2. It was a dark place with wild animals, mice, rats, and abject poverty. I saw Agido, a childhood friend of Theonoë's mother. She was tough, protective of her children, and alert for danger. I saw Anaktoria, yet another of her mother's friends. She was mean and hateful, also married but with only two kids. She was cynical and depressed. Then I saw Myrrhine, Theonoë's grandmother, in Thebes. Thebes was also still in ruins. It was a foul, cruel city, a center of robbery, murder, and debauchery. Myrrhine was a wild woman, copulating with deamons. She was filled with hatred, depressed and without morals. She had lost her humanity. And then I saw Athens. It was a place of dark political intrigue. It thrived but had become despotic toward its neighbors. It was hated in the islands. Theonoë learned this first when they arrived on Delos. They heard that Athens had forgotten the gods and not rebuilt the temples. "This is a Zeus civilization," an outraged Theonoë told them.

All in all, it was an extremely productive night using Active Imagination and dreams to explore my characters and storyline.

One more dream, and this one illustrates that what may seem a peripheral issue may in fact be a pivotal one. Here's the dream and what I wrote about it the next morning:

January 3, 2012

Last night I dreamed that I was walking somewhere among a group of students who were talking in a lounge, and one male student was telling a girl student about a text he had for one of his classes. I believe it was a novel, but the one thing that I remember most clearly is that the title of the text was Alph. *In my dream, the student had the paperback book in his hands, and the cover was plain, consisting of only large areas of different shades of dark green. The title* ALPH *was written in Arial font in all caps across the top of the cover. In the dream, I remembered having* Alph *as a text the previous semester, although I hadn't actually read it, or possibly read all of it. And either I remembered what it was about or the student was telling the girl about it.* Alph *had something to do with either a person inside a person or a social group within a social group, or*

Story Alchemy

a land within a land. It's really difficult for me to remember that much detail concerning the subject of the book.

When I woke this morning, I decided to see if such a book exists, so I went on Amazon and searched for the title, but only came across TinTin and Alph-Art. *Alph in this title actually applies to a shortening of the word alphabet, so this didn't seem to be a connection. Then I went on Wikipedia and searched for Alph.*

Alph turns out to be the name of the sacred river in Coleridge's poem Kubla Khan. *Some commentary concerning the poem considers the Alph to be a fictional river, but I would characterize it as mythological, which is a completely different perception when one uses an educated opinion of what mythology really is. Here is the complete poem* [added afterward] *as written in 1798:*

In Xanadu did Kubla Khan
A stately pleasure-dome decree:
Where Alph, the sacred river, ran
Through caverns measureless to man
Down to a sunless sea.
So twice five miles of fertile ground
With walls and towers were girdled round:
And there were gardens bright with sinuous rills,
Where blossomed many an incense-bearing tree;
And here were forests ancient as the hills,
Enfolding sunny spots of greenery.
But oh! that deep romantic chasm which slanted
Down the green hill athwart a cedarn cover!
A savage place! as holy and enchanted
As e'er beneath a waning moon was haunted
By woman wailing for her demon-lover!
And from this chasm, with ceaseless turmoil seething,
As if this earth in fast thick pants were breathing,
A mighty fountain momently was forced:
Amid whose swift half-intermitted burst
Huge fragments vaulted like rebounding hail,
Or chaffy grain beneath the thresher's flail:

Dream Invasion

And 'mid these dancing rocks at once and ever
It flung up momently the sacred river.
Five miles meandering with a mazy motion
Through wood and dale the sacred river ran,
Then reached the caverns measureless to man,
And sank in tumult to a lifeless ocean:
And 'mid this tumult Kubla heard from far
Ancestral voices prophesying war!
The shadow of the dome of pleasure
Floated midway on the waves;
Where was heard the mingled measure
From the fountain and the caves.
It was a miracle of rare device,
A sunny pleasure-dome with caves of ice!
A damsel with a dulcimer
In a vision once I saw:
It was an Abyssinian maid,
And on her dulcimer she played,
Singing of Mount Abora.
Could I revive within me
Her symphony and song,
To such a deep delight 'twould win me,
That with music loud and long,
I would build that dome in air,
That sunny dome! those caves of ice!
And all who heard should see them there,
And all should cry, Beware! Beware!
His flashing eyes, his floating hair!
Weave a circle round him thrice,
And close your eyes with holy dread,
For he on honey-dew hath fed,
And drunk the milk of Paradise.

    Although I do remember reading the poem for freshman English in 1960 and several times since, I haven't read the poem in decades and never had a conscious recollection of a river being in the poem, and certainly didn't remember Alph. I mostly remembered the pleasure dome. I wondered why this word "Alph" should now appear in my dream? And of course, my vampire novel came to mind.

The past couple of weeks or so, I've been working on a chapter where my little female vampire protagonist has had, for safety's sake, to join a colony of vampires in a vast network of caverns deep within the Carpathian Mountains of Romania. Just yesterday I was editing passages where she is to be initiated into the race of vampires. First she, along with other female and male vampires, bathes in a pond fed by an underground stream within the cavern to prepare for her initiation. Here is the text of two sentences as I left them yesterday: "A continuous stream of fresh water feeds the pool. It's simply an intermediate stop for water on its way to the lower chambers." Could it be that this was the impetus for my dream's reference to Coleridge's sacred river, Alph? Coleridge saw the poem in an opium-induced dream. It came to him as a finished work, although he only wrote down a portion of it before being interrupted and losing the rest. Could it be that I tapped into something within the Collective Unconscious related to this poem? Probably not. But what is even more interesting is what my Unconscious was trying to tell me and why it wrapped the subject matter within that fleeting reference to the Alph.

After considering this awhile, I've come to the conclusion that it is an answer to a problem I've been having trying to determine the location of my character's initiation. The Alph is a sacred river, so perhaps I should name my stream the Alph and have my little vampire initiated there in the stream or the pool created by it. Since it's sacred, the pond would be the place for the initiation, which would be similar to a baptism. I've also imagined music, and the Coleridge reference to a "damsel with a dulcimer" may be something further I can use. But I've noticed so many references in **Kubla Khan** that I relate to my vampire story that it is truly remarkable. I've already envisioned something I've called the "Vampire Wars" and here is Coleridge's reference to "Ancestral voices prophesying war!" But perhaps even the most remarkable connection is that of the "stately pleasure-dome." My vampires are always in pursuit of carnal experiences, and referencing orgies and characterizing this cavern or a portion of it as a palace of pleasure will do much to secure its identity.

Dream Invasion

Also, the antagonist of my story, and ruler over the race of vampires, is the original vampire who has lived for millennia and who was at one time a king or tribal warlord, somewhat of a Kubla Khan character.

I can scan this poem further for common elements and the way they are portrayed in Kubla Khan, *so that I might be able to breathe more life into the situations I've already envisioned for my vampire novel.*

The consequences of that dream and Coleridge's poem rippled through my novel. I might also add that in my dream the girl student who was being told about the book Alph was Lumi Laura, my narrator. She and I spent a lot of time incorporating images from the poem into the novel in the weeks and months following the dream.

Of course, my Unconscious by putting the word "Alph" on the cover of that book in my dream undoubtedly intended something additional. I used it for what first came to mind. I must remember that what comes from the Unconscious is intended as something compensatory for Consciousness being addressed not just at the novel but also toward me. I've not uncovered it yet, but tomorrow or years from now, I might find that additional meaning in that one simple fact from a dream. Evidently, it's an entire book on the Alph that was directed at me. Now that I think about it, the dream also led me to the concept of the Aleph, which I discussed toward the end of Chapter 6. All in all, a really productive dream.

One of the benefits of obtaining story material this way is that, since the material comes from the Unconscious, Consciousness has a connection, like Ariadne's thread, across the Transcendent Function to the location of the original material, and all of it may not have been mined in the dream. When this occurs, the process of editing the material can become extremely creative. Use your dreams as bridges to more story material in the Unconscious that may well be available during normal daytime editing.

★

Dream work is the most difficult to remember of all the techniques we've discussed. The story material uncovered is buried the most deeply within the Unconscious. The editing process helps to embed it in memory; however, writing a good story demands that we remember what has come before. How might we improve the situation? We have a bridge, the Transcendent Function, that helps, but we need much, much more than that. We need an entire psychic structure.

We need a memory palace.

CHAPTER 11 The Memory Palace

After discovering the Philosopher's Stone and applying many Jungian techniques to aid in its use, it might seem that the subject would be pretty well exhausted. Anything else of importance to help the author would be difficult to imagine. Well, get ready for another big one. I realize you won't be able to comprehend its significance at first, but you'll have to trust me on this. You haven't learned the most important thing. Not yet. I call it "the most important" somewhat in jest but also because it is the mechanism that populates the Imaginarium with your story and enables contemplation of it. This new discovery will weld your mind to the process. In many ways, it's what enables you to wield the Philosopher's Stone. It's known as "the memory palace."

And yes, it will also address the worthiness issue. Preliterate ancient Greek society measured a man by the quality and expanse of his memory. In a time when any thought, even those spoken, could vanish into thin air after the uttering, possibly never to be thought or heard again, memory was everything. For many occupations, including law, professional rememberers called mnemones were government officials and much in demand.

So here we go. Again.

Chances are you haven't thought about it, but one of

the greatest assets when writing an extended narrative is a good memory. By "memory" I'm specifically talking about remembering, instantly and without external aid, the details and structure of your story — its content and orchestration. When you hold details in Consciousness, it causes a scintillating effect something like viewing the primary stars of a constellation and watching the mind's eye create the associated image. If you look at the constellation Orion, you immediately see the four stars at the shoulders and knees, and that fuzzy band of stars in between that represents the belt and dagger, but your imagination then goes to work, and you intuitively start to envision the giant huntsman. Similarly, the more details of your story you can hold in your mind's eye at once, the more the story will build around them, and the better attuned they'll be to your needs.

Oral formulaic thought and expression ride deep in consciousness and the unconscious, and they do not vanish as soon as one used to them takes pen in hand. [Ong, page 26]

We also know that the mind never quits dreaming. Mental activity in the unconscious is continuous and ongoing, and the mind doesn't limit itself to just repeating what was put there but will ruminate on it, evaluate and revise it to suit itself relative to a higher form of knowledge in an even more remote psyche.

It's in fact much more important than that, and to reinforce how important it is, consider how memory helps form our own self-image. Here's what Joshua Foer, author of the 2011 non-fiction bestseller *Moonwalking with Einstein*, says about memory:

> *I thought of my own self fifteen years ago, and how much I've changed in the same period. The me who exists today and the me who existed then, if put side by side, would look more than vaguely similar. But we are a completely different collection of molecules, with different hairlines and waistlines, and, it sometimes seems, little in common besides our names. What binds that me to this me, and allows me to maintain the illusion that there is continuity from moment to moment and year to year, is some relatively stable but gradually evolving thing at the nucleus of my being.*

The Memory Palace

Call it a soul, or a self, or an emergent byproduct of a neural network, but whatever you want to call it, that element of continuity is entirely dependent on memory. [page 86]

Memory is crucial for a strong sense of self. We are mythical beings. We only know ourselves by memories of what we've done and what has happened to us. Those memories have formed through a sense of story. In an absolute sense, identity is the story of our lives. The way we put that story together is self-image. For a strong self-image, we need a series of well-defined successes throughout our own history. Memory is important almost beyond imagining. Here's more of what Joshua Foer has to say about it:

How we perceive the world and how we act in it are products of how and what we remember. We're all just a bundle of habits shaped by our memories. And to the extent that we control our lives, we do so by gradually altering those habits, which is to say the networks of our memory. ... Our ability to find humor in the world, to make connections between previously unconnected notions, to create new ideas, to share in a common culture: All these essentially human acts depend on memory. Now more than ever, as the role of memory in our culture erodes at a faster pace than ever before, we need to cultivate our ability to remember. Our memories make us who we are. They are the seat of our values and source of our character. ...memory training is not just for the sake of performing party tricks; it's about nurturing something profoundly and essentially human. [pages 269/270]

Although I may have some quibbles concerning how all-inclusive these statements are, I believe he's essentially correct that our self-identity is mostly dependent on memory. His statement that memory affects "How we perceive the world" has enormous implications for the creative writer of fictional worlds. What we remember of it determines how well we can imagine and describe it, and also how well our characters will function within it. This sounds an awful lot like the path to worthiness. We're always participating in the twin alchemical processes of becoming worthy while trying to transmute lead into gold.

Story Alchemy

Not only is the author dependent on memory when constructing the story, but the reader/viewer is also dependent on his/her own memory of what has happened in the story to make it come alive in the imagination. When you think about it, story is the time history of events, and if your audience can't remember what has happened, what is happening will make no sense, and what will happen will be of no importance. Plus, you lose the benefit of anticipation. Boredom sets in, and the reader will close the book or the audience will walk out of the theatre. You may think that the reader/viewer is responsible for what he/she remembers while reading or viewing the story, but that's just the author trying to shirk her/his responsibility toward the reader. The story can be constructed in such a way that it enhances the reader's memory. That's simply part of being a good storyteller — telling it so that you activate the reader's natural memory skills.

This is beginning to sound like I'm dumping a lot of responsibility on the shoulders of the author. Do we have any proof that techniques such as this have been used before and are effective? Well, how about Homer? Yes, the first great storyteller of Western Civilization used memory techniques that had been passed down from generation to generation for millennia. The basic stories behind *The Iliad* and *The Odyssey* were not the invention of Homer, who flourished around 700 BC. The stories of Achilles and Odysseus, who were undoubtedly real-life people and lived some 450 years earlier, came to him through an oral tradition. If you've ever read even a portion of these two epics, you realize that they are major creative works, extraordinarily complex, full of cultural traditions, religion, strange characters, spirits, gods, and violent action. What you will undoubtedly also notice is that they have a lot of repetition and other ticish characteristics that have puzzled scholars for millennia. What Homer did, as a part of the oral tradition, was to structure the story material with mnemonic devices to help him remember the events and their order. As Walter J. Ong put it, "[*The Iliad*] is built like a Chinese puzzle, boxes within boxes..." [*Orality and Literacy*,

The Memory Palace

page 27] Milman Parry first brought this to light back in the early part of the 20th century. Much of Homer's technique was apparent to his audience, and this also helped them understand and enjoy the story.

To appreciate the relationship between memory and the creative act, first realize that Mnemosyne, mother of all nine Muses, is the personification of memory. When we speak of "mnemonic" devices, we are unknowingly referring to the goddess. At the opening of Chapter 9, when we entered the Iris of Time and walked into the Imaginarium, the first person we encountered was Mnemosyne. So, first of all comes memory, and inspiration from the Muses, the daughters of Mnemosyne, follows in her train. All stories are in some way a mythology, the essence of which is stored away in the Unconscious.

It's the same with a novel, a play, or a movie. Even a video game. And here lies the secret of writing something that your reader can't put down. That "hook" at the beginning of a story that drags the reader/viewer/player in, in all seriousness, is nothing more than something that sticks in the memory and pulls the reader forward. The trick, of course, is how to do that effectively. Conflict, that upon which we have built our plot pentagon, has already tugged the reader into the future through that desire to know how the conflict is resolved. How do we get it to stick in the memory?

The author must work toward helping the audience remember what has come before, yet should not leave traces of his craft that aren't beneficial. C. S. Lewis put it this way:

> ...*all art is made to face the audience. Nothing can be left exposed, however useful to the performer, which is not delightful or at least tolerable to them.* [*A Preface to Paradise Lost*, page 19]

We have to make it irresistible to memory without making it obvious, and memory puts certain demands on what it wants to retain. We first have to solve this problem for the author and then also address how to help the audience without insulting their intelligence. Can we use Homer's technique? Probably not because it is too intrusive for today's tastes. We have another ancient Greek source for memory techniques that will serve us better. It was born of tragedy.

The poet Simonides of Chios (circa 500 BC) was at one time called out of a celebration, and just as he stepped outside, the building within which the celebration was being held collapsed, killing all inside. When family members came to claim their dead loved ones, the corpses were too mangled to identify. Simonides realized that he could remember where everyone was sitting by replaying his memory of the events in which each was involved. It seems that the mind is better at remembering spacial locations than facts. Plus, images are also easy to remember. Using location and events as memory aids, he showed each family member where to find their dead loved one. This technique became widely used throughout the ancient world, and has more recently come to be known as "the memory palace." Even though the origin of the technique has been historically attributed to Simonides, it may have actually come from Pythagoras, of all people, who would still have been alive when Simonides was young. The technique has never died out. It's used by many people today, and fuels the memories of international championship competitions.

The story of Simonides' discovery of the memory palace technique has traditionally come down to us through the writings of Cicero, but scholars today realize that the author of the *Rheortica Ad Horennium*, in which it is documented, is unknown. I've included the part of the *Rheortica Ad Horennium* that applies to the memory palace at the end of this book as Addendum I.

The importance of these memory techniques is also born out by a recent article in the New York Times. Three researchers, Dr. John O'Keefe, along with Dr. May-Britt Moser and her husband, Dr. Edvard I. Moser, have started decoding how memory works:

In 2005, they and their colleagues reported the discovery of cells in rats' brains that function as a kind of built-in navigation system that is at the very heart of how animals know where they are, where they are going

The Memory Palace

and where they have been. They called them grid cells.

...

On the most profound level, Dr. O'Keefe, the Mosers and others speculate that the way the brain records and remembers movement in space may be the basis of all memory. This idea resonates with the memory palaces of the Renaissance, imagined buildings that used spatial cues as memory aids. The technique dates to the ancient Greeks. In this regard, neuroscience may be catching up with intuition. [James Gorman, "A Sense of Where You Are," 4-29-2012]

It's quite possible that Socrates, a couple hundred years after Simonides, used a memory palace, or at least some form of mnemonic technique that served him well. Keep in mind that Socrates never wrote anything, and it would seem that he kept all his arguments in memory, possibly even composing them without benefit of stylus and waxed tablet. Perhaps Socrates' memory techniques made him the genius that he was. The surprising thing about it is that we have, through Plato of course, a firsthand account of Socrates in the act of exercising his mental process. Alcibiades, a prominent Athenian statesman, orator, and military general, describes what Socrates did for one twenty-four hour period while on active duty with the army during the Battle of Potidaea:

Well, so much for that. And now I must tell you about another thing 'our valiant hero [Socrates] dared and did' in the course of the same campaign. He started wrestling with some problem or other about sunrise one morning, and stood there lost in thought, and when the answer wouldn't come he still stood there thinking and refused to give it up. Time went on, and by about midday the troops noticed what was happening, and naturally they were rather surprised and began telling each other how Socrates had been standing there thinking ever since daybreak. And at last, toward nightfall, some of the Ionians brought out their bedding after supper — this was in the summer, of course — partly because it was cooler in the open air, and partly to see whether he was going to stay there all night. Well, there he stood till morning, and then at sunrise he said his prayers to the sun and went away. [*Symposium*, para 220c/d (page 571)]

It's entirely possible that not only was Socrates solving a philosophical problem, but that he was also executing a memory technique to store away this hard-won bit of wisdom so he could unleash it in one of his many dialogues with his compatriots.

Socrates' twenty-four hour meditation occurred in 432 BC, some 300 years after the Greeks adapted the Phoenician alphabet for their own language and started putting their greatest oral works on papyrus. Memory had been paramount for thousands of years, and when writing became available to record the stories, the entire oral culture started to shift to a literary one:

> *Homeric Greeks valued cliches because not only the poets but the entire oral neotic world or thought world relied upon the formulaic constitution of thought. In an oral culture, knowledge, once acquired, had to be constantly repeated or it would be lost; fixed, formulaic thought patterns were essential for wisdom and effective administration. But by Plato's day (427?-347BC) a change had set in: the Greeks had at long last effectively interiorized writing — something which took several centuries after the development of the Greek alphabet around 720-700 BC. The new way to store knowledge was not in mnemonic formulas but in the written text. This freed the mind for more original, more abstract thought.* [Ong, *Orality and Literacy*, page 23/4]

We have been living under that influence ever since. And it's a bigger change than you might think:

> *Without writing, the literate mind would not and could not think as it does, not only when engaged in writing but normally even when it is composing its thought in oral form. More than any other single invention, writing has transformed human consciousness.* [Ong, page 77]

Don't put too much stock on reading and writing as an aid to wisdom without storing much of it in memory. Here's what Thamus, King of Egypt, thought of writing, an opinion also subscribed to by Socrates:

The Memory Palace

And so it is that you, by reason of your tender regard for the writing that is your offspring, have declared the very opposite of its true effect. If men learn this, it will implant forgetfulness in their souls; they will cease to exercise memory because they rely on that which is written, calling things to remembrance no longer from within themselves, but by means of external marks. What you have discovered is a recipe not for memory, but for reminder. And it is no true wisdom that you offer your disciples, but only its semblance, for by telling them of many things without teaching them you will make them seem to know much, while for the most part they know nothing, and as men filled, not with wisdom, but with the conceit of wisdom, they will be a burden to their fellows. [Phaedrus 274e-275a, page 520]

Although you'll eventually see your story in print, treat these words of wisdom with the respect they deserve, and try to internalize and help your reader internalize your story by building the memory palace that will embed the memory of it in yours and your readers' psyches. And what I'm asking you to do is to revert back to 2500 year old techniques for supplemental assistance in creating your work of art.

Again, I know what you're thinking, and it's just not true. I can sense that you almost closed up this book and planned to never open it again. Everyone is afraid of difficult, painful memorizing techniques. But this one isn't difficult or painful. It's easy, and it's fun. Using this ancient Greek's memory aid, the memory palace, can turn practically anyone's mediocre memory into a world-class repository. According to Ben Pridmore, the 2004, 2008, and 2009 World Memory Champion, in conversation with Joshua Foer, "It's all about technique and understanding how the memory works. Anyone could do it, really." [page 7]

The good news is that we have already constructed our memory palace: the plot pentagon and dodecahedron. This is where you'll create the rooms, the spacial locations, to implant specific scenes from your story. It will even aid in bringing your story out of the mundane real world and into the mythical Land of Story. To remember something with a memory palace, you need locations, characters, and some associated weird activity. Strange behavior sticks in the memory better than the mundane.

It might help to view the exaggeration I'm recommending as being like a children's storybook. When you turn the pages, some of the images pop up and become three-dimensional. We need to accentuate some aspects of the story to make it memorable. Picking and pulling at details can make the entire scene come alive. This doesn't mean that you should take a gentle love story and make it into a sex manual. It takes a deft hand to accomplish some of this delicately, but on the other hand, some stories need the elevation of content through exaggeration to get at their essence.

Not only will this aid the writing of the story but also help the reader remember the storyline. The story builds in the reader's memory as it goes along, as it always does, but we're looking to make it vivid and unforgettable, something to crowd-out all other thoughts and encourage the reader to live in this fictional world. Let's again take a look at how Homer started out his epic poem. Imagine being in a dim candle-lit room crowded with people, you amongst them, seated for a long performance. The rhapsode sits before you readying himself. The audience turns quiet so that scarcely anyone breathes as his face lights up with inspiration, and then his voice rises into the air filling the room:

> *Sing in me, Muse, and through me tell the story*
> *of that man skilled in all ways of contending...*

A chill runs through you realizing that he has just called upon the goddess of epic poetry, Calliope, and that she has come amongst you to supply inspiration, and that he also has need of her mother, Mnemosyne, memory herself to guide him. He has constructed his material in such a way that it facilitates memory, but also aids the memories of those in his audience so that they might more fully understand and contemplate his story. Once his words evaporate into the air, they will be lost forever, unless the audience remembers them. Some will undoubtedly have memory skills of

The Memory Palace

their own and will be storing away his words for future reference. How might we go about accomplishing this ourselves? We start with building a memory palace. So what do they look like?

Memory palaces don't necessarily have to be palatial—or even buildings. They can be routes through a town... or station stops along a railway, or signs of the zodiac, or even mythical creatures. They can be big or small, indoors or outdoors, real or imaginary, so long as there's some semblance of order that links one locus to the next, so long as they are intimately familiar. [Foer, pages 96/7]

Here's where I make another confession. From the beginning, I've been leading you along the path to building a memory palace for your story. If, in our Imaginarium, we envision each of our five plot points as being "rooms" or "locations" wherein events take place, we then have the overall structure for retaining story details for these major milestones in the order in which they occur. The plot pentagon may not be a building, but it is a psychic storage "place" for the memory of events. The story structure, provided by the plot pentagon, connects the events. Here's the thing. We can use not only the plot pentagon but the entire dodecahedron as a plotting mechanism.

The dodecahedron contains a memory palace. To find it, we must set aside the idea that each of the pentagons that surround the central pentagon represents subplots. This illustrates a central aspect of the Philosopher's Stone. It's versatile and can be used in many different ways. It can be disassembled and its components put to various uses. You can use a single plot pentagon to explore a character arc or a subplot. You can use the second half of the dodecahedron, viewed from the antagonist's point of view, to research the antagonist's half of the story. If the storyteller has a need, the Stone can fulfill it, if he/she knows how to use it. Once you get used to working with it, you can always re-imagine it and find a solution to a new problem.

To build the memory palace, we go back to the flat construction-paper cutout that represented one half of the

Story Alchemy

dodecahedron. We can see that, between each plot point of the central pentagon, we can take a detour and go around the adjacent pentagon picking up three more plot points. This constitutes what I call a corridor. These contain the events that fall between plot points. Each segment, each corridor, contains three. Once we have identified our five major plot points, we can then fill in the fifteen corridor plot points. We have twenty total.

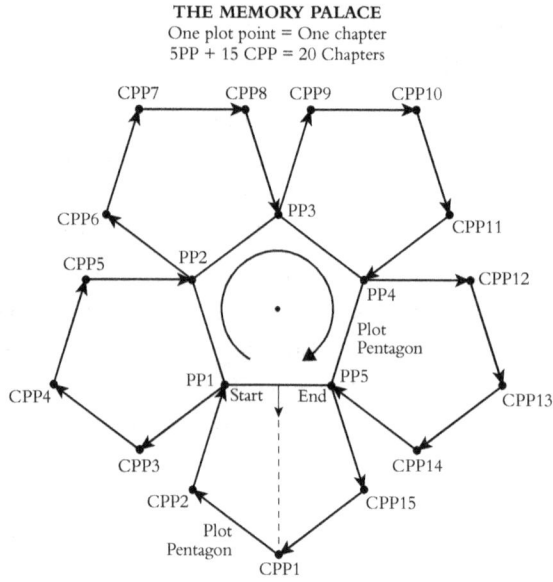

Figure 11-1 The Memory Palace

You can then trace the flow of the story, and it's not a storyline at all but a crooked path around all six pentagons, five external and one internal. This constitutes the memory palace for your story. It is in the overall shape of a downward-pointing pentagon.

Corridor events are different from central plot point events. They advance the story but don't actually turn the plot, at least not as much as do the central plot points. Initially you feel the urgency of the previous plot point pushing you forward, but as you approach the next plot point, you start feeling its pull. You navigate the pentagon as if pulled by gravity, and that gravity is the central conflict. We have three corridor plot point events for each line of the primary pentagon. For a novel, if we also view each vertex as a chapter, we then have twenty chapters. If we allocate fifteen pages for each chapter, the novel is 300 pages.

The excursions into the psyche to establish memory palace plot points are acts of colonization. We performed Active Imagination to get the plot points, and in doing so, the material within the plot points now resides in both Consciousness and the Unconscious by virtue of the bridge we have built between them. We have colonized part of the Unconscious with aspects of Consciousness.

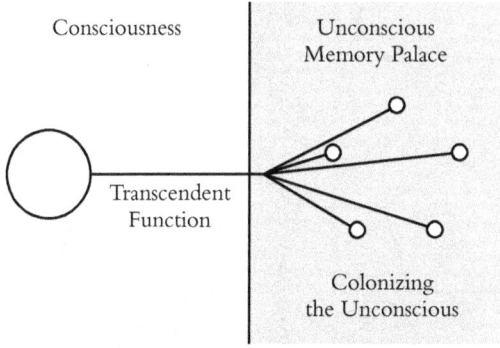

Figure 11-2 Colonizing the Unconscious

When we type our Active Imagination sessions, we are establishing a beachhead within the Unconscious that will enable us to reconnect with the Unconscious material while within Consciousness. Memory resides within the Unconscious. We don't know that we remember something until Consciousness accesses it, or requests the Unconscious through Mnemosyne to reveal it. When we are inside the dodecahedron, which resides within the Unconscious, we see all our little Consciousness colonies as plot points. All this is of course stored in our memory palace. The dodecahedron is not just a reference symbol. It is the active storage for the story.

Apparently, we can use the dodecahedron in any manner we wish. We can disassemble and use any part of it that serves our needs. If it's a particularly long story, we could also use one half of the disassembled dodecahedron as a memory palace for the first half of the story and the other half for the second half of the story. For a television series, each pentagon could represent an episode, and the complete dodecahedron for the overall series arc.

We can create a memory palace of all twelve pentagons, like this:

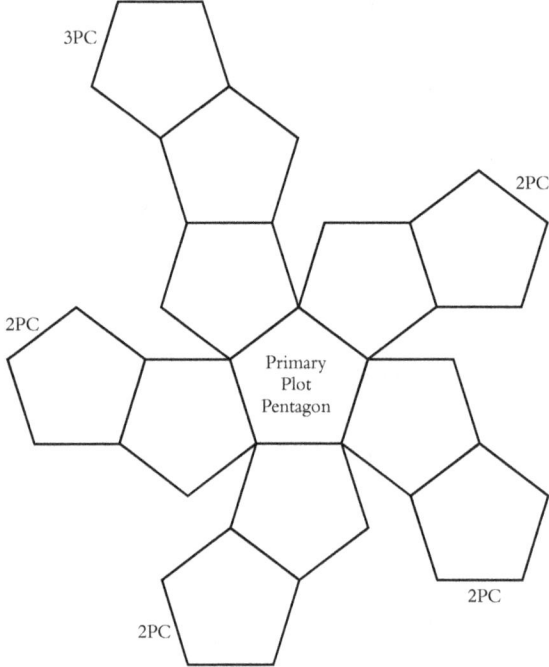

Figure 11-3 A Dodecahedron Memory Palace

At the top, right in the middle of the story, the stacked two-pentagonal corridors (2PC) become a stacked three-pentagonal corridor (3PC). We can devote this pentagon to the reversal (PP3). Once we memorize the basic twelve pentagonal pattern, we start loading each vertex (plot point and corridor plot point) with images and establish a path based on the proper sequence. That then represents your overall storyline. Once you envision your story as spanning the entire memory palace, all thirty-eight plot points, you'll feel the tension pull you through it.

Here's what you need to know to do that. First of all, load

The Memory Palace

each memory palace event (scene) with as many of the five senses as possible: sight, sound, feel, touch, and taste. Plus, you need to animate the image. Actions are easier to remember than stationary objects. Then you add one last touch: exaggeration, extraordinary beauty, debauchery, anything appropriate to the story that will take the action out of the ordinary. Memory stores the extraordinary, not the humdrum of daily life. This imbeds it in memory, but may also affect the nature of the scene and make it more interesting. You can allow some of this strangeness to infiltrate your story, but you must not allow it to disfigure the story too much. Take chances but still exercise a certain amount of control. Remember the one truism of all creative writing: life is stranger than fiction.

Initially you should throw caution to the wind. Here's what the author of *Ad Herennium* had to say about it:

When we see in everyday life things that are petty, ordinary, and banal, we generally fail to remember them, because the mind is not being stirred by anything novel or marvellous. But if we see or hear something exceptionally base, dishonourable, extraordinary, great, unbelievable, or laughable, that we are likely to remember a long time.

...

We ought, then, to set up images of a kind that can adhere longest in the memory. And we shall do so if we establish likenesses as striking as possible; if we set up images that are not many or vague, but doing something; if we assign to them exceptional beauty or singular ugliness; if we dress some of them with crowns or purple cloaks, for example, so that the likeness may be more distinct to us; or if we somehow disfigure them, as by introducing one stained with blood or soiled with mud or smeared with red paint, so that its form is more striking, or by assigning certain comic effects to our images, for that, too, will ensure our remembering them more readily. [See Addendum I]

Let's take a quick look at the Prologue of Dan Brown's novel *The Da Vinci Code* to see how he set up his story. In the opening, the curator of the Louvre in Paris pulls a large masterpiece off the wall to trigger an iron security gate that then descends to trap him inside but also prevents anyone access to where he is. Still, a man sticks a handgun through the bars and threatens to kill the curator if he doesn't reveal a certain secret for which he's come. The curator resists but eventually tells the gunman, an albino, what he wants to know. The albino shoots the curator in spite of the revelation, inflicting a fatal wound that will cause a painful death within a matter of minutes. The albino then leaves. But the curator did not tell the albino the truth, and if he doesn't leave some word behind, the secret will be lost forever. He then creates with his own blood a series of encrypted clues that can only be deciphered by one person, his granddaughter, and then only with the help of Professor Robert Langdon, the protagonist.

This is the setup for the most popular of Dan Brown's novels. You can easily see how it sticks in the memory by use of vivid images, unforgettable action, and a conflict that will span the entire novel. Simonides would have been proud. These are the keys to writing a bestselling novel, and Dan Brown didn't stop with the Prologue. Every scene of the novel contains all these same elements. They provoke the reader's interest and thus his/her memory.

Of course, *The Da Vinci Code* wasn't one of the finest pieces of literature ever written. Every story doesn't need this over-the-top action and images to bring it to life. Literary stories may be soft-pedaled and still retain the necessary ingredients. The opening sentence of Jane Austen's *Pride and Prejudice* is a good case in point:

> *It is a truth universally acknowledged, that a single man in possession of a good fortune, must be in want of a wife.*

This rather matter-of-fact sentence is simply loaded with the possibility of conflict and also sets a satiric tone that carries through the entire novel, which is a social comedy. One need not be overly dramatic to write a good story. You don't always have to have an albino committing a slow, painful and bloody murder. However, vivid images will always be of great assistance to your audience in remembering your story.

The Memory Palace

The ancient Greeks thought in memorable ways so they could remember what they mentally composed. This meant that

...you have to do your thinking in mnemonic patterns...Your thought must come into being in heavily rhythmic, balanced patterns, in repetitions or antitheses, in alliterations and assonances, in epithetic and other formulary expressions, in standard thematic settings... or in other mnemonic form. Serious thought is intertwined with memory systems. Mnemonic needs determine even syntax. [Ong, page 35]

Consonance, assonance, and alliteration as well as rhythm all play a part in the effectiveness of the first sentence of Jane Austen's *Pride and Prejudice* quoted above, particularly the last seven words: "...must be in want of a wife." Too much of this will give your prose a singsong quality that will quickly become objectionable. Yet, used with a deft touch, it can strengthen the emotional undertone and readily stick in your reader's memory.

One of the more effective ways to reinforce story structure in your own memory is to take a trip around your fictional world and reminisce about what has happened or will happen at each location. You can then use Active Imagination to find extraordinary details. This is similar to what tourists do with *The Da Vinci Code*. They go all over Paris and Rome seeking out the settings of various scenes from the book. If they can do that, you can do likewise with Active Imagination. You'll have to visit them in psychic space. If you're not interested in visiting these settings, neither will your audience. When you visit these places without the worry of trying to create story, you can simply enjoy being there and reminiscing about who did what where when and how. You'll also find details that you overlooked in the heat of telling the story and be able to find something that makes it more exotic. This is an excellent way of meditating on your story.

When you're walking around inside your story, you can sit on the same sofa where your protagonist turned her best friend and lover into a vampire. You can warm yourself before the fire where she used to sit worrying about how her life had crumbled. You can go outside and into the woods where she was first waylaid and became a vampire herself.

You have your plot pentagon to store the action and scenes of your story. All plot points and channels connecting them are containers for locations and actions. You can visualize this "cord of conflict" that runs through your story as a physical item that traverses these places. You can reflect on the event that locked the conflict at that first plot point. The setting is somehow "real" now, and when you consider it, wishing it to stick in yours and your readers' memories, you can stretch the strangeness and discover what that strangeness might be, what detail might take it out of the ho-hum world and bring it into the unusual so that you and your reader can better remember it. From there, you can take a walk around your plot pentagon. Doing this with each scene will make your story not only flow well but also make it unique and special.

Once you've done that with the central conflict, you can walk through this first plot pentagon, the Iris of Time, through the dodecahedron and over to the antagonist's plot pentagon. You then turn around and face back toward the protagonist's plot pentagon, which is now on the far side of the dodecahedron. It looks backwards and in disarray. The antagonists' plot pentagon looks right, and you can rewrite the premise and visit each plot point from his/her perspective. Perspective adds complexity. Your antagonist will no longer be so stereotypical. He/she'll acquire nuance, become more interesting, formidable. If they had a fight, you can see the same room where they fought, but if it was the protagonist's home, it now looks strange, foreign. You can feel the antagonist's intimidation at being in someone else's home. The uneasiness, fear. You can take the trip around this plot pentagon visiting all the plot points trying to understand what each event meant to the antagonist and uncover the Five Types of Deep Awareness that she/he must also experience.

Then you can go into the center of the dodecahedron, this three-dimensional bindu where the narrator resides, and talk to

The Memory Palace

your narrator, if it is a person, but also if it is just a presence that occupies the edge of the story. You can see the story from her/his/its perspective and look at each plot pentagon representing all the sub-conflicts from inside the dodecahedron. You can see how your narrator is orchestrating your story, perhaps even talk to him/her/it about it. You can talk to your minor characters. They don't have a large presence in your story, so they might enjoy a little one-on-one with the person channeling their words.

You can also look at the dodecahedron as the fictional world, with a sun, moon, stars. You can let the dodecahedron dissolve into the background and inhabit that world with its strangeness that comes from being only a world for the setting of your story. Now you can see more clearly how limited it is. If it's a world at war, you can feel the presence of the enemy, the great anger and fear destined to tear the countries apart. If it's a family feud, you can feel the hatred, the threat that hangs in the air like a heavy mist.

These are the imaginative tools you now have by using your plot pentagons and the three-dimensional dodecahedron as a representation of your story. You can use it as a memory palace and a creative tool. It is a mechanism for funneling psychic energy into your story. It is a visualization tool. It's the mechanism that grinds to life when your narrator starts telling your story. And it all resides inside your mind. It is a repository for your story, and you can work with it anytime you have a free minute. It also will enable you to get back into your story once you've been away from it for a while. Your mind has to reboot the story much like a computer rebooting its operating system. Having it instantly accessible by way of your memory palace will radically decrease this boot-up time, as if it's an entirely solid-state flash drive instead of one of the old mechanical, spinning-wheel hard drives.

You should also remember that each pentagon of your memory palace could be viewed as either a mandala or a yantra. You can read about their uses as meditation devices to gain more insight into the events that reside within your pentagons. You can also explore the all-encompassing circle to try to understand more about the philosophical implications of your story, the cosmic forces involved and the moral implications. You might even choose to take that dragon, the Ouroboros, from around the plot pentagon, release her so that she can come down to earth and talk to you about this story. She will have a perspective on it. You can also go into the center of the dodecahedron and focus on the sphere, that representation of God, and have a conversation with her/him about your story.

The plot pentagons, in both their mandala and yantra manifestations and the dodecahedron along with the all-encompassing sphere, are your Philosopher's Stone. It glows by virtue of the enlightenment emanating from the confluence of bindus. This is your mechanism through which you can visit your story in a way you've never before imagined. I have touched on some uses I've envisioned, but what I've presented is nowhere near exhaustive. The Philosopher's Stone now belongs to you. It's your instrument for creating and investigating your story. All it takes is a little Active Imagination to get the inspiration flowing.

You have the source of all creativity within you, and the evolutionary history of the human race resides there. It is a divine mechanism. Now that you've been handed the Philosopher's Stone, use it to unlock the mysteries of your fictional universe. It's specifically your tool for constructing and understanding the story you can't help but tell. More than that, it guides you along your own path to individuation and worthiness.

Realize that the basics of your story already existed before you found it. You are simply dressing it up in new clothes. If you can come to the point where you realize that your storytelling is not your creation but your discovery, you'll begin to truly understand the process. Remember, Jung said that even our thoughts do not belong to us. You have to give up the egotistical notion that you created the story. It is a gift, given to you by divine entities who reside within your Unconscious. They gave it to you because you are worthy. That must be enough to satisfy your ego.

This is the alchemy of storytelling.

CHAPTER 12 The Vampire Novel

After my first year experimenting with Active Imagination, I made a conscious decision to put the third volume of *The Mysteries*, the trilogy I was writing, on hold. I wanted a fresh project where I could start with new characters, a new narrator and a completely new storyline, so I could generate it using Active Imagination. I envisioned this project to be a young adult novel, something in what publishers call the "New Adult" genre, which is for late-teens, early-twenties readers. It was to be a vampire novel.

Why a vampire novel? I didn't examine my motives at the time, but I recently picked up the newly published, *Lament of the Dead*, a book of several conversations between the late James Hillman, who passed away in 2011, and Sonu Shamdasani concerning Jung's *The Red Book*. It spoke to me so loudly and on many levels, only one of which is that James Hillman is no longer with us. When I opened this book and read the first few lines, it took my breath away:

James Hillman: *I was reading about this practice that the ancient Egyptians had of opening the mouth of the dead. It was a ritual and I think we don't do that with our hands. But opening the* Red Book *seems to be opening the mouth of the dead.*

Sonu Shamdasani: *It takes blood. That's what it takes. The work*

Story Alchemy

is Jung's 'Book of the Dead.' His descent into the underworld, in which there's an attempt to find the way of relating to the dead. He comes to the realization that unless we come to terms with the dead we simply cannot live, and that our life is dependent on finding answers to their unanswered questions.

So it was for me with opening *Lament of the Dead*, for James Hillman spoke to me practically from the grave. His and Shamdasani's words rippled through my perception of my own vampire novel as I read them, not only because Hillman is no longer with us and we are still trying to come to terms with him and the loss of him, but also because I'm getting along in years myself, and my vampire book also reflected more emphasis on the questions of mortality and immortality. That, and since it was to be generated using Jung's Active Imagination, which is of course a process of descending into the underworld, my vampire novel was definitely a book of the dead also, or the undead.

And then I realized that it was much more than even that. I first ran onto Hillman's work at the suggestion of Renate Wood some twenty-five years ago. I was struggling with Sophocles' *Oedipus at Colonus* (another story of descent into the underworld), and she recommended that I take a look at a little volume titled *Oedipus Variations* written by both Hillman and Kerenyi. I was blown away by the depth of Hillman's understanding of Sophocles. Dr. Wood was my mentor, and the gifts she gave me so unassumingly continue to speak to me today. One of them led me to this book. I could still hear her speaking from the grave, and the way she came to me was as a background voice, someone looking over my shoulder and whispering between-the-lines secrets as I read the words of Hillman and Shamdasani.

I was much more primed for my vampire novel than I knew. It was to be quite short. Something I could complete in a couple of months. Shouldn't be too difficult for a seasoned novelist and non-fiction author, I reasoned.

Don't I wish.

Two years into the project, it was still going strong. The

The Vampire Novel

problem was that the technique worked much better than I anticipated, and the story was more interesting and sophisticated. I was impressed by the complexity of its spiritual and intellectual underpinning. Granted, I was also writing this book, *Story Alchemy*, in parallel while also contributing to several blogs, but still, the story was surprisingly engrossing as was the Active Imagination techniques I was developing. I was gaining so much insight into the creative process that I couldn't resist letting the vehicle I was using for insight grow beyond its original scope.

I tried what I believed to be an original approach to creating the narrator. I stretched the concept to its limit by envisioning her as a "real" person currently living in Romania, the setting for my story. Since she's the one who was to give all the words to me, I gave her a pen name and a life, all of which I developed through Active Imagination. Actually, I didn't give her anything. She just stepped forward and told me about herself. To write the novel, I crossed over into the Imaginarium and visited her in Romania. You can visit her too. She has a blog where she tells about her "life" and keeps her readers up to date on her writing projects. Just search on "Lumi Laura."

Her novel also has a website where she presents previews of chapters and associated short stories concerning her characters. It's titled *Carpathian Vampire, ...when you've never known love....* Her protagonist is a young woman (Alexandra Eidyn) of eighteen, who reluctantly becomes a vampire, but she also has family, friends, enemies, and at times it's difficult to tell which is which. In working with all this, I first cleared my psychic space, walked through the Iris of Time into the Imaginarium, gathered these psychic entities about me, and then typed the words that came to me through Lumi.

As I mentioned earlier, I got the idea for a vampire novel at about the same time I had the dragon dream. Perhaps the dream was the initial shove into vampire territory. Anyway, I used Active Imagination from the beginning to develop even the idea and the outline (plot pentagon). Ninety percent of all the material came from Active Imagination.

As you can imagine, it's not a pure process. One of the things about the Unconscious is that you don't find a lot of specifics there. I have had names come to me through Active Imagination, but that isn't generally the way specifics surface. I think that, with more practice, I could uncover more detailed information, but it's a little like seeing images. It takes practice within psychic space. I believe the same is true with facial features. We don't see them by default but have to make a specific effort.

To find a location for the events of Lumi Laura's story, I went on the Internet. Sinaia appeared to be an interesting place. Queen Marie had lived there. Sinaia, the monk who founded it, Queen Marie and the man with whom she had an affair, Alex Eidyn as Queen Marie's great great granddaughter, the vampire mythology — all one neat package. It seemed to be all connected in psychic space and had been from the beginning.

And this raises an interesting question. When we think we are working alone, are these psychic entities still there in the background making decisions for us? Are we deluding ourselves thinking we have any autonomy? I believe the answer is that they are always there and always influencing us. Lumi seemed to be influencing me from the very beginning, even before she came to me in psychic space. When I found the little mountain town of Sinaia and thought it an excellent place to set my vampire story, was Lumi Laura working in the background by manipulating my sensibilities to resonate with it? I think so. Otherwise, Sinaia wouldn't have been so serendipitously connected with the rest of the story. It all fits together like a jigsaw puzzle.

I also looked for Romanian names that she could use for herself and her characters. Through a combination of my research and her inspiration, we gradually came to an understanding. I then started Active Imagination sessions about the actual story. Lumi realized that her protagonist, who went by Alex, had no intention of become a vampire even though she wasn't very satisfied with her own life. When she was turned, that immediately put her

The Vampire Novel

in conflict with the person who turned her, a conflict that was to span the length of the novel. Alex also had to come to terms with herself as a vampire, and this is an internal conflict that also is resolved at the end, or at least comes to some sort of truce. I used the Iris of Time and the Imaginarium to sort through the structure of the multitude of conflicts involved.

Since one of her antagonists is the first vampire, Lumi felt that she needed to present more about the history of the race of vampires. She brought forward a mythology that goes back over three-thousand years and beyond to the Garden of Eden, having it would seem consulted the Divine World of the sphere. It's all quite ingenious — the way she interwove mythology, religion and her own take on how it all happened. Originally, she intended the vampire mythology to be short stories that would only be published separately, but they were so unusual and well formed that I encouraged her to open the novel with two of them. This essentially stretched the setup to three chapters instead of one. It all seems so theatrical. What a great way to open a movie, should it ever be picked up for the big screen.

Since I was researching methods for *Story Alchemy* while writing *Carpathian Vampire*, not all the methods I developed were available while I was writing the initial chapters, and it would have been impossible to redo the entire novel with what I knew at the end. I also had no intention of starting a new novel specifically to try out these methods. I will use them to write the third volume of my trilogy, *The Mysteries: The Twice-Born*.

But I couldn't publish *Carpathian Vampire* without using the memory palace techniques, so I went back through the vampire novel by way of the Iris of Time, met up with Lumi Laura using Active Imagination, and took another look at some scenes, realizing I had to ensure they were memorable both for the reader and me. I returned to the *Rhetorica Ad Herennium* for methods.

Another thing I realized was that I had two major plotlines running simultaneously, and neither could be considered a subplot. To structure this unusual situation, I generated two superimposed plot pentagons. One represented my protagonist's conflict in the real word and the other her conflict with entities from the Divine World. Some plot points from different pentagons occurred in separate chapters, but other plot points from different pentagons occurred in the same chapter. This wasn't something Lumi and I planned. It just turned out that way. I generated a memory palace for each.

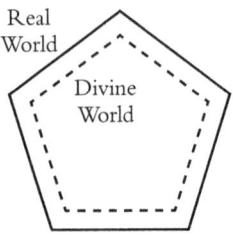

Figure 12-1 Parallel Plot Pentagons
Real World — Divine World

This emphasizes the point that you can disassemble the dodecahedron for use in any way that delineates story structure. Nothing is pure in this business, and you should adapt the plotting aids to fit the story you are telling. Stories are inherently so complex that you have to be creative in your use of the Philosopher's Stone. It will always provide insight into story arc whether it's a scene in a play, chapter in a novel, or an episode of a television series. All the events of the story-unit you are investigating will then have cause-and-effect relationships and philosophical depth.

For the vampire story, I was particularly interested in using images and actions that would add humor. For this, I looked to irony. Irony is the source of practically all humor. (See *Novelsmithing*, Chapter 5.) So Lumi and I went back through the novel and transformed each scene, when we thought it necessary, into something more memorable. I then tested it on myself by asking how well each scene stuck in my memory. I made sure that I could go through the story from memory, scene by scene. Since *Carpathian Vampire* has fifty-two chapters, my memory palace consisted of both halves of the dodecahedron, plus some modifications.

The main thing I learned from using Active Imagination to write *Carpathian Vampire* is to trust and believe in the process. Even though you will give your novel a broad outline using the plot pentagon, all sorts of subplots will cluster about it and shoulder their way into your story. Sometimes the story will take off in directions that you hadn't intended in the beginning. Trust these and work with them. Having an overall concept for the story should gradually drag these diversions back into the main stream of your story. How far to let them drag it off the beaten path? Well, that's your call. It's not an exact process. As a matter of fact it's really messy, and that's the way it should be.

I can't imagine writing a novel using my old methods. Lumi and I may write a second volume of *Carpathian Vampire* in the not too distant future. But I'm also interested in getting back to writing the third volume of *The Mysteries, The Twice-Born*. Plus, I have other stories starting to bubble up from my Collective Unconscious. Having the Philosopher's Stone seems to unleash the elements of story from within my imagination, and some of them are really off the wall. It's as if the characters know that I now have the skill to bring their stories to life and can't wait to get them told. Perhaps some sort of resonance occurs with these untold stories and the presence of the Philosopher's Stone that resides also in the Collective Unconscious as well as Consciousness by virtue of the Transcendent Function. This of course is because they exist in a state of perpetual conflict, and that's an unstable state, and they wish to have their conflicts resolved. Remember that old adage about letting sleeping dogs lie? We'll, if you've read this book, you woke them up, and now you've got to deal with them. The good news is that you now have the tools.

★

For those interested, I've provided one of my active imagination sessions in raw form as Addendum II. I've included the process of entering the Iris of Time, greeting my narrator, Lumi Laura, and taking dictation from her. This session occurred on August

1, 2011. We accomplished quite a lot that night. Again, I've not edited it, so you can see it in the rough. I'd prepped myself thoroughly beforehand so that I knew exactly where I was in the story relative to my plot points and what I wanted to get out of it. Still yet, the conversation flowed as if I were streaming a Netflix movie. The narrative, of course, comes in the voice of my author/narrator, Lumi Laura. It's one of my better Active Imagination sessions, with me typing on a Bluetooth keyboard in total darkness. It was one continuous session with no break. In the novel, this particular event occurs in Chapter 21: Encounter with Father Zosimos.

★

The greater portion of this book, *Story Alchemy*, also came from Active Imagination. It was given to me, and I wrote it in a matter of only three months, plus of course a few more months for editing. It is a subject that has plagued me for the better part of forty years. Even more than writing stories, I have wanted to understand the art of storytelling. One thing I know with absolute certainty: I understand only a fraction of all the wisdom contained in the Philosopher's Stone. It's as if the process exposed itself through me and not necessarily because it is meant for my use. Perhaps it is meant for you, my readers, and I am but a messenger. If it is meant for you, you will recognize it and be able to wield it. If not, you'll shrug your shoulders and talk off, perhaps even have a good chuckle at all the shenanigans I suggest just to get some words on the page. For those who recognize its worth and are willing to spend the time it takes to learn the process, it could be the missing link that has held you back from expressing what is in your soul.

I have compared what we have discovered here in *Story Alchemy* to that of the technology of the ancient Krell in the classic sci-fi movie *Forbidden Planet*. Although the Krell became technologically advanced almost beyond imagining, they destroyed themselves because they had forgotten something that was a part of their psychological makeup from the beginning of their millions of years of evolution: the base nature that comes from the Id — their

The Vampire Novel

own greed, lust and hatred. Their Ids took over their ability to spontaneously project anything their minds could conceive into the real world. Storytelling is such a technology. The Krell turned on each other. Their entire civilization vanished in a single day.

Forbidden Planet was a work of art and not something taken from actual events in the real world. Adam Adler conceived the story; Cyril Hume wrote the screenplay. However, Adler confessed that he had adapted Shakespeare's play *The Tempest* for the storyline, although one could well imagine that even *The Tempest* had its origin in Sophocles' *Oedipus at Colonus*. It seems to be one of those stories that resurfaces under another guise in a different time but always to serve as a reminder that human beings are forever flawed, and the sin of arrogance is always punished.

The Id is a concept that comes from Freudian psychology and not from Jung. It is the result of a more pessimistic view of human nature, but one we would do well to keep in mind. I will not allow myself into certain areas of psychic space, or perhaps I should say that I will not permit contact with certain personages there. I sense something I call the Great Evil with whom I will not form even a psychic relationship. You might consider this and question whether everything within you should be brought into the world. All culture is projected from psychic space into the real world, a process that has its analog with ancient Krell technology. Jung thought we should be careful with what we bring out. I believe that is good advice.

The Iris of Time isn't a one-way conduit. What you bring out with you may not always be what you think. And what you bring doesn't come in a box and isn't an inanimate object. One might compare what I have given you to Pandora's Box. These are intelligent psychic beings with thoughts of their own.

During the two and one half years of practicing Active Imagination to channel Lumi Laura's *Carpathian Vampire*, I came across several instances where the material went beyond what I consider my own personal boundaries for the presentation of violence and sex in literature intended for young people ages

Story Alchemy

16 to 25 but also possibly of interest for all adults. Some of her language in Chapter 3 To Grandmother's House concerning her protagonist's physical attributes prior to becoming a vampire seemed too crass. I let this pass. The first of the instances that truly bothered me was in Chapter 9 An Unfortunate Encounter where Ms Laura's protagonist is attacked by a rapist. Her reaction to the attack and her subsequent actions, her violence and sexual aggressiveness, went far beyond what I would have written by my usual creative methods. Even in other areas of less concern, I didn't agree with what she'd written. I started to edit it out, but then thought I should at least try to maintain the integrity of the process by honoring her perspective.

My apprehension dramatically escalated in Chapter 29 The Pleasure Dome when her protagonist was initiated in a vampire psychic location called Millennium Road. The problem was that this scene is reprised even more dramatically close to the end of the novel in Chapter 47 Battle of Pivniţă de Vinuri. I had pulled the scene in The Pleasure Dome back to something I thought I could tolerate only to learn that the even more graphic material later on demanded that the earlier material be reinstated. It seems that Ms Laura knew what she was doing all along. I felt that I was being played. I was concerned about my reputation as an author, and it was obvious that she didn't see me as the ultimate authority on her story. This was when I decided to publish it under her name and not my own. Do I think that absolves me of responsibility for the nature of the material in the novel? Obviously not. But still...

You must realize that yours are not just benign fantasies but real psychic entities from the Collective Unconscious. They animate us and provide content in story form. Once turned loose upon the world, your story is no longer a part of you. The work goes its own way. You lose control, and they can do good or wreak havoc as they please. Psychic beings from your Collective Unconscious are then activated in the psychic world of your readers, and within this new moral context, they may find expression in the real world. This is the reason, as the ancient alchemists realized, for the worthiness issue. [Jung, *The Red Book*, page 291]

At the end of *Forbidden Planet*, the human visitors to that ancient world blew up Altair, the home planet of the ancient Krell, thus destroying all the knowledge they had developed. The commander of the starcruiser didn't believe that beings on planet Earth were ready for such knowledge. They weren't worthy. I've given you a tool that may be as powerful as anything the Krell developed. Be mindful how you use it.

★

Storytelling is a universal part of human existence. This could lead one to believe that the Philosopher's Stone might not be just for storytellers. It is the way we resolve conflict, both internal and external. Its use is therapeutic as shown by its relationship to Jung's Transcendent Function. It is operative all the time helping create the human narrative. We live our life story, creating it along the way. As Joshua Foer says, we are our memories, and our memories beget stories, just as Mnemosyne is the mother of the Muses. We are mythic beings.

Now that you've spent some time with the Philosopher's Stone, you should step back a little and see what you've accomplished, or perhaps what you will accomplish through this process. To learn to wield the Philosopher's Stone, you'll have to attain a certain level of personal perfection. And this is in psychic space, which we've pretty much agreed has a relationship with the Divine World. We've not specifically striven for eternal life, but it seems that it's always an issue when you're dealing with the Stone. We've not really addressed it as being the Elixir of Life, the giver of immortality. But an alchemist would have thought of it in this light. Since we've used Jung's technique for becoming individuated, you'll perfect your soul to a certain extent. It may not bring you to the point of eternal life here in the real world, but if we listen to the alchemists whose path we've been following, you very well may give yourself a better chance of obtaining it in psychic space or, as we sometimes call it, the Afterlife.

THE END

Addendum I

Excerpt from
Rhetorica Ad Herennium
(English: 'Rhetoric: For Herennius')
Author unknown, ~90s BC (formerly attributed to Cicero)
Published in the Loeb Classical Library, 1954
Translated by Harry Caplan
The text is now in the public domain.

[This is our best account of the method of memorization attributed to Simonides of Chios, who flourished around 500 BC. It is a mnemonic technique historically known as "the method of loci" but popularly called "the memory palace."]

Now let me turn to the treasure-house of the ideas supplied by Invention, to the guardian of all the parts of rhetoric, the Memory.

The question whether memory has some artificial quality, or comes entirely from nature, we shall have another, more favourable, opportunity to discuss. At present I shall accept as proved that in this matter art and method are of great importance, and shall treat the subject accordingly. For my part, I am satisfied that there is an art of memory — the grounds of my belief I shall explain elsewhere. For the present I shall disclose what sort of thing memory is.

There are, then, two kinds of memory: one natural, and the other the product of art. The natural memory is that memory which is imbedded in our minds, born simultaneously with thought. The artificial memory is that memory which is strengthened by a kind of training and system of discipline. But just as in everything else the merit of natural excellence often rivals acquired learning, and art, in its turn, reinforces and develops the natural advantages, so does it happen in this instance. The natural memory, if a person is endowed with an exceptional one, is often like this artificial memory, and this artificial memory, in its turn, retains and develops the natural advantages by a method of discipline. Thus the natural memory must be strengthened by discipline so as to become exceptional, and, on the other hand, this memory provided by discipline requires natural ability. It is neither more nor less true in this instance than in the other arts that science strives by the aid of innate ability, and nature by the aid of the rules of art. The training here offered will therefore also be useful to those who by nature have a good memory, as you will yourself soon come to understand. But even if these, relying on their natural talent, did not need our help, we should still be justified in wishing to aid the less well-endowed. Now I shall discuss the artificial memory.

The artificial memory includes backgrounds and images. By backgrounds I mean such scenes as are naturally or artificially set off on a small scale, complete and conspicuous, so that we can grasp and embrace them easily by the natural memory — for example, a house, an intercolumnar space, a recess, an arch, or the like. An image is, as it were, a figure, mark, or portrait of the object we wish to remember; for example, if we wish to recall a horse, a lion, or an eagle, we must place its image in a definite background. Now I shall show what kind of backgrounds we should invent and how we should discover the images and set them therein.

Those who know the letters of the alphabet can thereby write out what is dictated to them and read aloud what they have written. Likewise, those who have learned mnemonics can set in backgrounds what they have heard, and from these backgrounds deliver it by memory. For the backgrounds are very much like wax tablets or papyrus, the images like letters, the arrangement and disposition of the images like the script, and the delivery is like the reading. We should therefore, if we desire to memorize a large number of items, equip ourselves with a large number of backgrounds, so that in these we may set a large number of images. I likewise think it obligatory to have these backgrounds in a series, so that we never by confusion in their order be prevented from following the images — proceeding from any background we wish, whatsoever its place in the series, and whether we go forwards or backwards — nor from delivering orally what has been committed to the backgrounds. For example, if we should see a great number of our acquaintances standing in a certain order, it would not make any difference to us whether we should tell their names beginning with the person standing at the head of the line or at the foot or in the middle. So with respect to the backgrounds. If these have been arranged in order, the result will be that, reminded by the images, we can repeat orally what we committed to the backgrounds, proceeding in either direction from any background we please. That is why it also seems best to arrange the backgrounds in a series.

    We shall need to study with special care the backgrounds we have adopted so that they may cling lastingly in our memory, for the images, like letters, are effaced when we make no use of them, but the backgrounds, like wax tablets, should abide. And that we may by no chance err in the number of backgrounds, each fifth background should be marked. For example, if in the fifth we should set a golden hand, and in the tenth some acquaintance whose first name is Decimus, it will then be easy to station like marks in each successive fifth background. Again, it will be more advantageous to obtain backgrounds in a deserted than in a populous region, because the crowding and passing to and fro of people confuse and weaken the impress of the images, while solitude keeps their outlines sharp. Further, backgrounds differing in form and nature must be secured, so that, thus distinguished, they may be clearly visible; for if a person has adopted many intercolumnar spaces, their resemblance to one another will so confuse him that he will no longer know what he has set in each background. And these backgrounds ought to be of moderate size and medium extent, for when excessively large they render the images vague, and when too small often seem incapable of receiving an arrangement of images. Then the backgrounds ought to be neither too bright nor too dim, so that the shadows may not obscure the images nor the lustre make them glitter. I believe that the intervals between backgrounds should be of moderate extent, approximately thirty feet; for, like the external eye, so the inner eye of thought is less powerful when you have moved the object of sight too near or too far away.

Although it is easy for a person with a relatively large experience to equip himself with as many and as suitable backgrounds as he may desire, even a person who believes that he finds no store of backgrounds that are good enough, may succeed in fashioning as many such as he wishes. For the imagination can embrace any region whatsoever and in it at will fashion and construct the setting of some background. Hence, if we are not content with our ready-made supply of backgrounds, we may in our imagination create a region for ourselves and obtain a most serviceable distribution of appropriate backgrounds.

On the subject of backgrounds enough has been said; let me now turn to the theory of images.

Since, then, images must resemble objects, we ought ourselves to choose from all objects likenesses for our use. Hence likenesses are bound to be of two kinds, one of subject-matter, the other of words. Likenesses of matter are formed when we enlist images that present a general view of the matter with which we are dealing; likenesses of words are established when the record of each single noun or appellative is kept by an image.

Often we encompass the record of an entire matter by one notation, a single image. For example, the prosecutor has said that the defendant killed a man by poison, has charged that the motive for the crime was an inheritance, and declared that there are many witnesses and accessories to this act. If in order to facilitate our defence we wish to remember this first point, we shall in our first background form an image of the whole matter. We shall picture the man in question as lying ill in bed, if we know his person. If we do not know him, we shall yet take some one to be our invalid, but a man of the lowest class, so that he may come to mind at once. And we shall place the defendant at the bedside, holding in his right hand a cup, and in his left tablets, and on the fourth finger a ram's testicles. In this way we can record the man who was poisoned, the inheritance, and the witnesses. In like fashion we shall set the other counts of the charge in backgrounds successively, following their order, and whenever we wish to remember a point, by properly arranging the patterns of the backgrounds and carefully imprinting the images, we shall easily succeed in calling back to mind what we wish. When we wish to represent by images the likenesses of words, we shall be undertaking a greater task and exercising our ingenuity the more. This we ought to effect in the following way:

Iam domum itionem reges Atridae arant.

"And now their home-coming the kings, the sons of Atreus, are making ready."

If we wish to remember this verse, in our first background we should put Domitius, raising hands to heaven while he is lashed by the Marcii Reges — that will represent "Iam domum itionem reges" ("And now their home-coming the kings,"); in the second background, Aesopus and Cimber, being dressed as for the rôles of Agamemnon and Menelaüs in Iphigenia — that will represent "Atridae parant" ("the sons of Atreus, making ready"). By this method all the words will be represented. But such an arrangement of images succeeds only if we use our notation to stimulate the natural memory, so that we first go over a given verse twice or three times to ourselves and then represent the words by means of images. In this way art will supplement nature. For neither by itself will be strong enough, though we must note that theory and technique are much the more reliable. I should not hesitate to demonstrate this in detail, did I not fear that, once having departed from my plan, I should not so well preserve the clear conciseness of my instruction.

Now, since in normal cases some images are strong and sharp and suitable for awakening recollection, and others so weak and feeble as hardly to succeed in stimulating memory, we must therefore consider the cause of these differences, so that, by knowing the cause, we may know which images to avoid and which to seek.

Now nature herself teaches us what we should do. When we see in everyday life things that are petty, ordinary, and banal, we generally fail to remember them, because the mind is not being stirred by anything novel or marvellous. But if we see or hear something exceptionally base, dishonourable, extraordinary, great, unbelievable, or laughable, that we are likely to remember a long time. Accordingly, things immediate to our eye or ear we commonly forget; incidents of our childhood we often remember best. Nor could this be so for any other reason than that ordinary things easily slip from the memory while the striking and novel stay longer in mind. A sunrise, the sun's course, a sunset, are marvellous to no one because they occur daily. But solar eclipses are a source of wonder because they occur seldom, and indeed are more marvellous than lunar eclipses, because these are more frequent. Thus nature shows that she is not aroused by the common, ordinary event, but is moved by a new or striking occurrence. Let art, then, imitate nature, find what she desires, and follow as she directs. For in invention nature is never last, education never first; rather the beginnings of things arise from natural talent, and the ends are reached by discipline.

We ought, then, to set up images of a kind that can adhere longest in the memory. And we shall do so if we establish likenesses as striking as possible; if we set up images that are not many or vague, but doing something; if we assign to them exceptional beauty or singular ugliness; if we dress some of them with crowns or purple cloaks, for example, so that the likeness may be more distinct to us; or if we somehow disfigure them, as by introducing one stained with blood or soiled with mud or smeared with red paint, so that its form is more striking, or by assigning certain comic effects to our images, for that, too, will ensure our remembering them more readily. The things we easily remember when they are real we likewise remember without difficulty when they are figments, if they have been carefully delineated. But this will be essential — again and again to run over rapidly in the mind all the original backgrounds in order to refresh the images. I know that most of the Greeks who have written on the memory have taken the course of listing images that correspond to a great many words, so that persons who wished to learn these images by heart would have them ready without expending effort on a search for them. I disapprove of their method on several grounds. First, among the innumerable multitude of words it is ridiculous to collect images for a thousand. How meagre is the value these can have, when out of the infinite store of words we shall need to remember now one, and now another? Secondly, why do we wish to rob anybody of his initiative, so that, to save him from making any search himself, we deliver to him everything searched out and ready? Then again, one person is more struck by one likeness, and another more by another. Often in fact when we declare that some one form resembles another, we fail to receive universal assent, because things seem different to different persons. The same is true with respect to images: one that is well-defined to us appears relatively inconspicuous to others. Everybody, therefore, should in equipping himself with images suit his own convenience. Finally, it is the instructor's duty to teach the proper method of search in each case, and, for the sake of greater clarity, to add in illustration some one or two examples of its kind, but not all. For instance, when I discuss the search for Introductions, I give a method of search and do not draught a thousand kinds of Introductions. The same procedure I believes be followed with respect to images.

Now, lest you should perchance regard the memorizing of words either as too difficult or as of too little use, and so rest content with the memorizing of matter, as being easier and more useful, I must advise you why I do not disapprove of memorizing words. I believe that they who wish to do easy things without trouble and toil must previously have been trained in more difficult things. Nor have I included memorization of words to enable us to get verse by rote, but rather as an exercise whereby to strengthen that other kind of memory, the memory of matter, which is of practical use. Thus we may without effort pass from this difficult training to ease in that other memory. In every discipline artistic theory is of little avail without unremitting exercise, but especially in mnemonics theory is almost valueless unless made good by industry, devotion, toil, and care. You can make sure that you have as many backgrounds as possible and that these conform as much as possible to the rules; in placing the images you should exercise every day. While an engrossing preoccupation may often distract us from our other pursuits, from this activity nothing whatever can divert us. Indeed there is never a moment when we do not wish to commit something to memory, and we wish it most of all when our attention is held by business of special importance. So, since a ready memory is a useful thing, you see clearly with what great pains we must strive to acquire so useful a faculty. Once you know its uses you will be able to appreciate this advice. To exhort you further in the matter of memory is not my intention, for I should appear either to have lacked confidence in your zeal or to have discussed the subject less fully than it demands.

THE END

Addendum II

Raw Active Imagination Session

(Typos and all.)

Here in its entirety I've provided one of my better Active Imagination sessions. I've included the process of entering the Iris of Time, greeting my narrator, Lumi Laura, and taking dictation from her. This session occurred on August 1, 2011. It is not edited. I'd prepped myself thoroughly beforehand so that I knew exactly where I was in the story relative to my plot points and what I wanted to get out of it. Still yet, the conversation flowed as if I were watching a movie on Netflix. The narrative, of course, comes in the voice of my author/narrator, Lumi Laura. Here it is typos and all.

I see the lady in white pacing back and forth on the balcony. I approach her and she immediately turns back into thehome, walks through the living room and into the antiroom and hands the key to the Guardian of the Gate. i acknowledge her and she turns the key in the mechanism so that the ir Iris slides silently open. I see Lumi on the tripod.

They [the three protagonists: Alexandra, Jaklin, and Mikhail] entered the monastery grounds from a parking lot where tourists parked, and they walked through up the steps and into the new chapel. They found a monk in the far corner inspecting a painting of Carol I. Alex asked if he knew how they might find Father Zosm Zosimos.

And who may I say whiches to see him?

Alexandra Eidyn, she said.

Oh, my , yes, he said. Follow me please.

They left the chapel through the back door, crossed chapel ground to the old to a row of rooms along the side of the square. past the old chaptel Alex knew was built in sixxteen eighty five. They stopped out from of one of the doors, and he asked them to wait there, and he'd see if Father Zosimos could would be avilable.

Alex felt displaced here at the monastery. She felt little of its religious

Raw Active Imagination Session

significance. This was suposed to be holy gru ground, and yet, the gazebo seemed more sacred to Alex. She looked at Jaklin and Mikhail. "I feel so foolish," she said. "I wish I hadn't come."

But the monk returned just then, and Father Zosimos was following behind.

"My dear young lady," he said. What a pleasant surprise, and I see you've brought two friends with you?

Yes, Father. They are the de dearest friends in th all the world to me. I have something important to discuss with you, and I want them present.

then let us find suitable quarters, he said., and he led them away from the row of room and to another chapel where he entered and led them down the id isle where he seated them in the first row and brought up a chair so that he might face them.

Alex noticed that that the cross that Christ's cross, large and intimidating stood in the background behind him.

He motioned for her to talk.

I've a confession, she started, and looked down at her folded hands. She pulled her from from within her blouse, so that she might gain the courage from it she needed to tell this story. First I must tell you the humilitating news that I am pregnant.

And who is the father of ? he asked glancing quickly at Mikhail.

I've had a paternity check, and although it could be Mikhail, it isn't. but the other sad news is that a few weeks ab ago, I was raped It was just before you came to test me of for vampireism with the crosses.

My child, did your grandmother know i of this?

No. No onw one but me knows about this until just now. I There's a great deal more to the story that you should all her hear. Perhaps you should just let me tell it all, and then you can do with me as you whish.

Please, then. I be quite. Proceed.

You've all heard of the serial rapist that was murdered in the park. Well, it was he s who raped me. Since the child does not beli belong to Mikhail, I can only say that it must be the rapist's child I carry.

Father Zosimos makes an exp exclamation.

I know that you tested me with the cross and proved to your satisfaction that I'm not a vampire, but I know myself that I am one, *butcause when he raped me, I attac I turned on him with such ferocity an I can only compare it to that of a while whild animal. I am the one who murdered him while he was in the act of raping me. I sucked every ounce of blood from his body, and such was my hunger for blood that once I had drained him, I attacked the other man right there in the park. It's a wonder that I didn't kill him too. I realize that I don't fit the mold of a normal vampirebut as I told you before, and also have told Jaklin and Mikhail, I was bitten by a woman who sucked my blood. I was told by a divine being nmaed Catalin that the woman was a divine being. he told me that I wouldn't become a vampire unless I drained killed a human being by sucking their bllo blood, which I did.*

"*So you see father, I am a vampire, and I have to have blood from time to time, and I go out at night, when I can get away from Jaklin and Mikhail without their knowing, and I find someone to feed on. I've don e done it several time, and I'm afraid that I'm causing much of the hysterial now raging in Sinaia.*

So here's my question father. I feel that I should hav have the child. I don't want to end its little life. It is half me, but how can I have the child of a sesrial rapist?

Father Zosimos started to speak but then fell silent. She Alex could see tears in her eyes. Finally he spoke. Why weren't you wearing the corss, he said. You promised.

But father, I was wearingt the cross when he raped me. Why didn't it protect me?

Enough! girl. Pl Please! shouted Father Zosimos. Such profane things spoken here before our Lord in his own temple. I know such things as though you speak exist because I've seen them with my own eyes. But never would one of them enter such holy ground as this. He turned to Jaklin. Have you seen any of this. Do their of you, and he looked a Mikhail know this to be true? Is she delusional?

She is not delusional, said Jaklin. Yet she only gives you the sorry side of her condition. forjust a few night ago, we witnessed what is all but a miracle performed by Missy.

Missy? Who is this Missy?

That's the name Alex gave to us as her own nmae. We've know her

Raw Active Imagination Session

as Missy from the first.

Go on. Tell me of the miracle.

We were taken to a pla home where Missy was requested to allow a vampire to bite her. This she did, and her blood cured the person of his vampirism. And then another also' And then another also, added Mikhail. She was a wonder. Even the two people whose home it was claim to have been turned bc back from vampireism previously. She has a gift. but these new revelations of rabid vampirism herself, and murder. I've not hear of this. He glanced at Alex but immediately averted his eyes, as if finding a repusle repulsion in the very site of sight of her.

And this relationship between the three of you, what is the nature of it?

the room fell silent, none of them wishing to allow anyone to share their secret.

Finally, Jaklin answered. We love her, she said. It's just quite simply tu true. We love her.

Is it carnal, the pris priest asked.

Yes, Father, said Mikhail. I'm afraid it is.

Father Zosimos rose from his chair and paced about the room a bit. 'Yet another plus to this perrible afliction is that those off of whom I feed are inoculated from ever having the vampire's disease. The other man I bit on the night I committed the murder, he was bitten again but has never become a vampire. I am not a normal vampire. It has to do with Velinar, the woman who bit me, that divine being.

Okay. that is enough. I get the picture, said Father Zosimos. I have a de tendency to be lenient in the human failing of the follower of Christ's followers, But this goes beyond anything of which I have knowledge. Yet, one this seems an absolute certainty. The nature of who you are, and the lifestyle you've chosen, say to me that that you must give up the cross. That which I gave to you should not bring comfort to one who practices such acts.

But oh Father, I do so love this cross. Ples please don't take it from me.

Then promise me that yo will give up these two friends of your, and that you will no longer feed off the blood of other human beings.

But Father. It's not a choice. It's a compulsion. I have no more control over it that than I do breathing. And I do them no harm.

Do they voluntarily give up their blood to you?

Alex looked away from his eyes and felt great shame. No Father. I take it by force.

As I thought. And this relationship   carnal relationship with your two friends?

They are beyond a compulsion. I love them oboth so completely that I would give them up no more than I would christ.

Is this not lust that drives your need for them? Is it not the carnal part of the relationship that draws you to them?

I don't deny that that the act is a great joy of mine. But the true essence of my feeling for them is the the love and compassion they show me. Their great kindness and affection for me. Their concern for me. That and their compassion for all things that live on this earth and the love of life here.

And yet are they practicing Christians. are you a practicing Christian.

No Father, not in the sense that we belong and participate in the church. But the way they live their lives is in the true traditions and path shown by Christ's life and teachings.

Yes, well the carnal nature of yor your relationsip would seem to show a different side of that story, wouldn't it.

Perhaps, Father.

Handm me the cross, child. I'll have it back.

But oh Father. It will break my heart ot to do so.

He reached out his hand.

A great sadness rose up inside Alex as she raised the golden chain from around her neck and ove her head. You'll have to take it from me, she said. For I cannot give it up of my own free will.

With that he reached for it, but she would not turned it loose.

Please, f Father.

Relax your fingers.

She did and felt her cross leave her possession. She cried.

Now, about the child you carry within you. It is a great relief to hear you say that you wish to carry it to full term. It is God's child, and to end

Raw Active Imagination Session

it wold in itself be murder. That you worked this out yourself is a great comfort to me and tells me that you are not beyond hope. but I must tell you, and this may also be your choice. You cannot raise the child. It will should be given to those who can give it a proper family.

The thought of giving up the child was a grief she cu could not bear. Oh, non, Father. I already have a great affection for the child. I love. surely that will be my continual act of contrition, to see to its wellbeing always.

But it is not your comfort and desire, your feeling that should be considered in this but only that of the child, the best situation for the child. Surely you can see that being raised by a vampire is not in its best interest?

T Ath those words, Alex broke. something inside her seemed to crack open and all the grief sadness and grief flowed into her soul, and she cried great sobs. Like great gusts of a hurricane the missery of the soul pounded her being.

Jaklin held her all the way back t home, but Mikhail was distant, quiet, and kept a pace or two from them.

I'm losing him, Alex thought. He is such a fine young man, and I've lost him.

Catalin will tell Alex that the cross is not only from the wood of Christ's cross, but it is also from the Tree of Life out of the Garden of Eden. It would be be a great crime to take the cross from her because it is from the fruit of the tr Tree of Life that she gains her immortality here on Earth. She is destined to live forever, and it is because of the Tree of Life. Catalin also denies that her relation with both Jaklin and Mikhail is profane. This is not lust. Love is what God puts in our hearts to work the great good in the world. If they share this love for you, then it is one of God's great earthly mysteries and must be honored.

But I've already lost Mikhail, Alex tells him. He's drifted from me.

Love has its great moments, but it also ebbs and flows. Yes, he may grow distant from you for a time, but if it is the love you've described to me, perhaps it will return.

The session ends as the sounds of Lumi's voice and the visions fade. I walk back through the Iris, thank the Guardian of the Gate and hear it quietly slide shut behind me. Once again I'm home in my bed, and it *is the middle of the night.*

So that's what one of my better Active Imagination sessions, with me typing on a Bluetooth keyboard in total darkness, looked like. It was one continuous session with no break. In the novel, this particular event occurs in Chapter 21: Encounter with Father Zosimos.

THE END

Bibliography

Aristotle, *The Complete Works of Aristotle* (Two Volumes), ed. by Jonathan Barnes, Princeton: Princeton University Press, 1984.

Blacker, Irwin R., *The Elements of Screenwriting*, New York: Longman, 1986.

Borges, Jorge Luis, *Collected Fictions*, tr. by Andrew Hurley, New York: The Penguin Group, 1998.

Burroway, Janet, *Writing Fiction, A Guide to Narrative Craft*, New York: Addison Wesley Longman, 2000.

Calame, Claude, *The Craft of Poetic Speech in Ancient Greece*, tr. by Janice Orion, Ithaca: Cornell University Press, 1995.

—, *Poetic and Performative Memory in Ancient Greece, Heroic Reference and Ritual Gestures in Time and Space*, Washington: Center for Hellenic Studies, 2009.

Egri, Lajos, *The Art of Dramatic Writing, Its Basis in the Creative Interpretation of Human Motives*, New York: Simon & Schuster, 1960 (1946).

Eliade, Mircea, *The Myth of the Eternal Return*, tr. by Willard R. Trask, Princeton: Princeton University Press, 1971 (1954).

—, *Patterns in Comparative Religion*, tr. by Rosemary Sheed, Lincoln: University of Nebraska Press, 1958.

—, *Rites and Symbols of Initiation, The Mysteries of Birth and Rebirth*, Putnam: Spring Publications, 1994.

—, *The Sacred and the Profane, The Nature of Religion*, tr. by Willard R. Trask, New York: Harcourt, Inc., 1957.

Field, Syd, *Screenplay, The Foundations of Screenwriting*, New York: Dell Publishing, 1994.

Foer, Joshua, *Moonwalking with Einstein, The Art of Remembering Everything*, New York: The Penguin Press, 2011.

Fontana, David, *Meditating with Mandalas*, London: Duncan Baird Publishers, 2005.

Freytag, Gustav, *Technique of the Drama, An Exposition of Dramatic Composition and Art*, tr. by Elias J. MacEwan, Chicago: Scott,

Foresman & Company, 1900.

Guthrie, W.K.C., *Orpheus and Greek Religion, A Study of the Orphic Movement*, Princeton: Princeton University Press, 1952.

Hannah, Barbara, *Encounters with the Soul*, Wilmette: Chiron Publications, 1981.

Hesiod, *Hesiod: Theogony, Works and Days, Shield*, tr. by Apostolos N. Athanassakis, Baltimore: The Johns Hopkins University Press, 1983.

Hillman, James, *Archetypal Psychology, A Brief Account*, Dallas: Spring Publications, 1983.

—, *Healing Fiction*, Putnam: Spring Publications, 194 (1983).

—, & Sonu Shamdasani, *Lament of the Dead, Psychology after Jung's Red Book*, New York: W. W. Norton & Company, 2013.

Johnson, Robert A., *Inner Work: Using Dreams and Active Imagination for Personal Growth*, San Francisco: HarperSanFrancisco, 1986.

Jung, C.G., *The Archetypes and the Collective Unconscious*, tr. by R.F.C. Hull, Princeton: Princeton University Press, 1959.

—, *Aion, Researches into the Phenomenology of the Self*, tr. by R.F.C. Hull, Princeton: Princeton University Press, 1959.

—, *Alchemical Studies*, tr. by R.F.C. Hull, Princeton: Princeton University Press, 1967.

—, *Children's Dreams, Notes from the Seminar Given in 1936-1940*, ed. by Lorenz Jung and Maria Meyer-Grass, tr. by Ernest Falzeder, Princeton: Princeton University Press, 2008.

—, *Dreams*, tr. by R.F.C. Hull, Princeton: Princeton University Press, 1974.

—, *Jung on Death and Immortality*, selected and with an intro. by Jenny Yates, Princeton: Princeton University Press, 1999.

—, *Jung on Active Imagination*, ed. and with an intro. by Joan Chodorow, Princeton: Princeton University Press, 1997.

—, *Jung on Alchemy*, ed. and with an intro. by Nathan Schwartz-Salant, Princeton: Princeton University Press, 1995.

—, *Jung on Evil*, ed. and with an intro. by Murray Stein, Princeton: Princeton University Press, 1995.

—, *Mandala Symbolism*, tr. by R.F.C. Hull, Princeton: Princeton

Bibliography

University Press, 1969.
—, *Memories Dreams, Reflections*, ed. by Aniela Jaffe, tr. by Richard and Clara Winston, New York: Vintage Books, 1989.
—, *Mysterium Coniunctionis*, tr. by R.F.C. Hull, Princeton: Princeton University Press, 1963.
—, *The Practice of Psychotherapy*, tr. by R.F.C. Hull, Princeton: Princeton University Press, 1966.
—, *Psychology and Alchemy*, tr. by R.F.C. Hull, Princeton: Princeton University Press, 1968 (1953).
—, *The Red Book*, ed. and with an intro. by Sonu Shamdasani, tr. by Mark Kyburz, John Peck, and Sonu Shamdasani, New York: W.W. Norton & Company,
—, *The Red Book, A Reader's Edition*, ed. and with an intro. by Sonu Shamdasani, tr. by Mark Kyburz, John Peck, and Sonu Shamdasani, New York: W.W. Norton & Company, 2009.
Khanna, Madhu, *Yantra, The Tantric Symbol of Cosmic Unity*, Rochester: Inner Traditions, 2003 (1979).
Kübler-Ross, Elizabeth, *On Death and Dying*, New York: Macmillan Publishing Co., Inc., 1969.
Liminality and Transitional Phenomena, ed. by Nathan Schwartz-Salant and Murray Stein, (The Chiron Clinical Series) Wilmette: Chiron Publications, 1991.
Llinas, Rodolfo R., *I of the Vortex, From Neurons to Self*, Cambridge: MIT Press, 2001.
LaBerge, Stephen, *Lucid Dreaming, The Power of Being Awake & Aware in Your Dreams*, New York: Ballantine Books, 1985.
—, *Exploring the World of Lucid Dreaming*, New York: Ballantine Books, 1990.
Laura, Luminita (Lumi), *Carpathian Vampire, When You've Never Known Love*, Healdsburg: Tragedy's Workshop, 2014.
Mazur, Joseph, *The Motion Paradox, The 2,500-Year-Old Puzzle Behind All the Mysteries of Time and Space*, New York: Dutton, 2007.
McKee, Robert, *Story, Substance, Structure, Style, and the Principles of Screenwriting*, New York: ReganBooks, 1997.
Miller, Jeffrey C., *The Transcendent Function*, Albany: State University

of New York Press, 2004.

Ong, Walter J., John Hartley, *Orality and Literacy*, New York: Routledge, 2002 (1982)

Plato, *Plato, The Collected Dialogues*, ed. by Edith Hamilton and Huntington Cairns, Princeton: Princeton University Press, 1961.

Riedweg, Christoph, *Pythagoras, His Life, Teaching, and Influence*, tr. by Steven Rendall, Ithaca: Cornell University Press, 2002.

Shelley, Mary, *Frankenstein*, Mineola: Dover Publications, Inc., 1994 (1831).

Sheppard, David, *Novelsmithing, The Structural Foundation of Plot, Character, and Narration*, Healdsburg: Tragedy's Workshop, 2009.

Stein, Murray, *In Midlife*, Putnam: Spring Publications, 2003 (1983).

—, *Jung's Map of the Soul*, La Salle: Open Court Publishing, 1998.

—, *Transformation, Emergence of the Self*, College Station: Texas A&M University Press, 1998.

von Franz, Marie-Louise, *Alchemical Active Imagination*, Boston: Shambhala, 1997.

—, *Interpretation of Fairy Tales*, Dallas: Spring Publications, Inc., 1970.

Walter, Richard, *Essentials of Screenwriting, The Art, Craft, and Business of Film and Television Writing*, New York: The Penguin Group, 2010.

Yates, Francis A. *The Art of Memory*, London: Pimlico, 1966.

Index

A

Abraham, F. Murray 75
Achilles 152
Active Imagination iv, vii, 76, 80, 81, 82, 85, 86, 87, 90, 91, 95, 97, 98,
    100, 101, 102, 103, 104, 105, 107, 108, 109, 110, 111, 115, 120, 121,
    122, 123, 125, 126, 127, 128, 129, 132, 134, 135, 137, 138, 141, 142,
    143, 161, 165, 168, 169, 170, 171, 172, 173, 175, 176, 177, 188, 194,
    196, 198
Adler, Adam 177
Agony of Choice 29
Alchemical Active Imagination 97, 198
Alcibiades 155
aleph 78
Aleph 78, 147
Alice and Wonderland 65
Alph 143, 144, 146, 147
Amadeus 75
Apostles 73
A Preface to Paradise Lost 153
Aquinas, St. Thomas 49
Archetypal Psychology 117, 196
Archetypes 58, 124, 196
Ariadne 105, 147
Aristotle 7, 8, 27, 28, 29, 55, 116, 195
Art of Dramatic Writing, The 23, 195
Aubuchon, Remi 18
Austen, Jane 164, 165
author iv, 13, 14, 22, 31, 39, 45, 58, 59, 62, 67, 68, 69, 75, 76, 77, 83, 84,
    85, 86, 87, 88, 91, 92, 94, 95, 116, 118, 119, 120, 121, 122, 123, 124,
    127, 128, 131, 132, 137, 141, 149, 150, 152, 153, 154, 163, 170, 176,
    178, 188
awareness 39, 52, 85, 93, 94, 95, 99, 105, 138

B

Battle of Potidaea 155
Battlestar Galactica 18
Becoming Worthy vii, 80 (Chapter 7)

Bendton, Robert 21
bindu 47, 48, 49, 50, 51, 52, 55, 75, 79, 99, 103, 115, 123, 166
Bindu Radiation 50
bindus 168
Black Hole 135
Blacker, Erwin R. 7, 23, 29
Bluetooth Keyboard 108, 176, 194
Borges, Jorge Luis 78, 195
Bowie, David 17
Brown, Dan 163, 164
Buddha 93
Buddhas 55, 94
Buddhism 44, 48
Buffy the Vampire Slayer 19, 46
Burroway, Janet 7
Byron, Lord 62, 81

C

Calliope 158
Cameron, James 30, 97
Caprica 18
Carpathian Vampire 171, 173, 174, 175, 177, 197
Chaos vii, 13, 79
Children's Dreams 110, 132, 196
Chodorow, Joan 82, 196
Christ 49, 73, 129, 130, 189, 191, 192, 193
Christian 88, 192
Clooney, George 21
Coleridge, Samuel 129
Collective Unconscious 58, 59, 61, 63, 64, 65, 66, 75, 77, 78, 80, 85, 98,
    99, 104, 106, 117, 124, 129, 137, 139, 146, 175, 178, 196
Conflict 16, 18, 21, 24, 25, 26, 90, 92, 93, 153
Consciousness iv, 56, 58, 81, 84, 85, 86, 87, 88, 89, 90, 96, 98, 105, 109,
    110, 111, 112, 116, 118, 120, 121, 125, 126, 127, 128, 129, 132, 133,
    147, 150, 161, 175

D

dead 95, 169, 170, 196
denouement 31, 33, 44, 83, 91, 141
Da Vinci Code, The 163, 164, 165
da Vinci, Leonardo 49

Index

dialogue 90
Dillard, Annie 7
Disney 18, 19
Divine World 39, 65, 78, 173, 174, 179
dodecahedron 71, 72, 73, 75, 76, 77, 78, 88, 113, 114, 115, 120, 123, 141, 157, 159, 160, 161, 162, 166, 167, 168, 174
dragon 44, 51, 53, 54, 55, 76, 94, 96, 103, 134, 168, 171
Dream Invasion vii, 131, 133, 136
Dreams 105, 110, 124, 130, 132, 133, 136, 196, 197

E

Egri, Lajos 23
Egyptians 44, 169
Einstein, Albert 6
Einstein-Rosen Bridge 51
Elements of Screenwriting, The 23, 195
Eliade, Mircea 102
Elixir of Life 5, 88, 179
Escape of Bobby Ray Hammer, The 131
Event Horizon 134, 135, 137

F

Fairytale 64
fantasy 82, 83, 117, 119, 141
Field, Syd 7, 14, 28, 29
Five Types of Deep Awareness 93, 166
Foer, Joshua 150, 151, 157, 159, 195
Fontana, David 55, 56, 195
Forbidden Planet 98, 99, 102, 176, 177, 179
Force, The 97
Frankenstein 62, 80, 101
Franklin, Jon 27
Freud, Sigmund 12, 58, 59, 80
Freytag, Dr. Gustav 40

G

God 37, 38, 77, 130, 168, 192, 193
Gospel of Thomas 88
Greeks 36, 38, 44, 71, 77, 155, 156, 165, 186
Groundhog Day 29

H

Hall, James A. 120
Hanks, Tom 19
Hansel and Gretel 65
Hermes 101
Hillman, James 117, 169, 170, 196
Hinduism 44, 47
Hippasus of Metapontum 72
Homer 106, 152, 153, 154, 158
Hulce, Tom 75
Hume, Cyril 177

I

iCloud 108
Iliad, The 152
Imaginarium 115, 116, 117, 118, 120, 121, 122, 123, 130, 133, 149, 153, 159, 171, 173
individuation 10, 88, 91, 93, 95, 168
In Midlife 105, 198
iOS 108
iPad 108
iPhone 108
Iris of Time vii, 52, 100, 101, 104, 111, 113, 118, 119, 120, 122, 125, 132, 133, 134, 135, 136, 137, 139, 142, 153, 166, 171, 173, 175, 177, 188
Isaacson, Walter 18

J

James, Henry 7
Jaws 30
Jedi Knight 97
Jobs, Steve 18
Jung, Carl Gustav iv, 9, 10, 12, 13, 14, 44, 47, 56, 57, 58, 59, 61, 75, 80, 81, 82, 83, 84, 85, 86, 87, 88, 89, 90, 91, 96, 97, 103, 110, 119, 122, 124, 125, 127, 132, 141, 168, 169, 170, 177, 179, 196, 198
Jungian iii, iv, 9, 75, 81, 85, 91, 117, 149
Jung on Active Imagination 82, 196
Jung on Alchemy 196

K

Katzenberg, Jeffrey 18

Index

Keeper of the Gate 106
Khanna, Madhu 48, 52, 53, 197
King, Stephen 7
Kramer vs. Kramer 21
Krell 99, 102, 176, 177, 179
Kubla Khan 144, 146, 147
Kübler-Ross, Elizabeth 41

L

LaBerge, Stephen 136
Lament of the Dead 169, 170, 196
Land of Forgetting 107
Land of Myth 35
Land of Not Knowing 107
Land of Story vii, 35, 47, 77, 102, 112, 113, 121, 157
lapis 86
Lasseter, John 18, 19
Last of the Mohicans, The 30
Lewis, C. S. 153
liminal 104, 105, 106, 111, 119, 123, 130
liminality 104, 105, 119
Liminality and Transitional Phenomena 102, 106, 119, 197
Lord of the Rings, The 25
lucid dreaming 130, 133, 136
Luke Skywalker 97
Laura, Lumi 147, 171, 172, 173, 174, 175, 176, 177, 188, 193, 197

M

mandala 44, 51, 54, 55, 56, 66, 67, 68, 88, 93, 95, 102, 123, 125, 132, 167, 168
Matrix, The 45, 65
Matthew 130
Mazur, Joseph 39, 197
McKee, Robert 7
meaning iv, 23, 25, 32, 38, 51, 65, 66, 71, 74, 92, 93, 104, 120, 147
memory 82, 107, 112, 114, 116, 117, 123, 131, 135, 137, 148, 149, 150, 151, 152, 153, 154, 155, 156, 157, 158, 159, 160, 161, 162, 163, 164, 165, 167, 173, 174, 180, 181, 182, 184, 185, 186, 187
memory palace 148, 149, 154, 155, 157, 159, 160, 161, 162, 163, 167, 173, 174, 180
Miller, Jeffrey C. 86, 90, 197

Mnemosyne 113, 116, 153, 158, 161
Moonwalking with Einstein 150, 195
Moore, Robert L. 102, 105
Moore, Ron 18
Moser, Edvard I. 154
Moser, May-Britt 154
Mozart 75
Muse 106, 158
Muses 114, 116, 119, 153
Mysteries, The 142, 169, 173, 175, 195
Mysterium Coniunctionis 9, 13, 82, 96, 119, 141, 197

N

Narnia 120
narrator 67, 75, 76, 77, 95, 114, 115, 116, 118, 119, 122, 123, 124, 127, 139, 142, 147, 166, 167, 169, 171, 175, 176, 188
Newton, Sir Isaac 6, 7, 8, 10, 34, 38, 77, 78
nigredo 5, 6
Novelsmithing iv, 8, 9, 174, 198

O

Obi-Wan Kenobi 97
Odysseus 152
Odyssey, The 106, 152
Oedipus 9, 170, 177
Oedipus at Colonus 170, 177
Oedipus on a Pale Horse 9
O'Keefe, John 154
Olympian gods 73
Olympian Zeus 77
On Death and Dying 41
On Memory 116
Ong, Walter J. 152
Orality and Literacy 152, 156, 198
uuroboros (uroboros) 44, 54, 55, 76, 94, 95, 96, 103, 115, 134, 168

P

Parmenides 65
Patterns of Comparative Religions 102
pentagon 33, 34, 35, 36, 37, 38, 39, 40, 43, 44, 47, 49, 50, 51, 54, 55, 56, 66, 67, 68, 70, 71, 72, 73, 75, 76, 77, 89, 90, 91, 95, 102, 103, 113,

Index

114, 115, 123, 153, 157, 159, 160, 161, 162, 166, 167, 168, 171, 175
pentagram 35, 36, 37, 44, 47, 49, 50, 51, 55, 72, 93, 103, 123
Periodic Table of the Elements 72
Perks of Being a Wallflower, The 17
Personal Unconscious 57, 58, 59
Phaedrus 157
Rhyme of the Ancient Mariner, The 129
Philosopher's Stone i, iv, vii, 1, 3, 5, 6, 7, 8, 9, 10, 12, 43, 44, 46, 66, 67, 76, 78, 81, 82, 87, 88, 89, 108, 114, 115, 149, 159, 168, 174, 175, 176
Phoenician alphabet 156
Pixar 18, 19
Plato 44, 65, 71, 155, 156, 198
Plot iv, vii, 27, 31, 35, 52, 68, 70, 90, 174, 198
Plot Diagram 52
Plot Pentagon vii, 27, 68, 70
Plot Points 31
Poetics 7, 27, 28
Poincaré Dodecahedral Space 73
point-of-view character 69, 74
Pride and Prejudice 164, 165
prima materia 5, 13, 15, 50, 63, 79, 81, 88, 96
psychology iii, iv, 8, 47, 62, 86, 91, 97, 104, 117, 177
psychotherapist 97
Pythagoras 36, 39, 51, 72, 154, 198
Pythagoreans 36, 71, 72, 73, 77, 78

R

Rapunzel 65
Red Book, The 80, 125, 169, 197
religion 26, 37, 47, 56, 73, 77, 106, 128, 152, 173
rhapsode 158
Rheingold, Howard 136
Rheortica Ad Horennium 154
Riedweg, Christoph 72, 198
Rocky Mountain Writers Guild 8
Romania 146, 171
Romeo and Juliette 64

S

Salieri 75

Schultz, William Todd 12
Schwartz-Salant, Nathan 102, 106, 119, 196, 197
screenwriting iv, 16
serpent 44
setup 17, 31, 33, 44, 90, 102, 132, 138, 164, 173
sex 16, 80, 158, 177
Shadow iv, 6, 57, 58, 59, 61, 64, 65, 85, 88, 96, 98, 106
Shamdasani, Sonu 169, 170, 196, 197
Shelley, Mary 62, 80, 81, 83, 101
Simonides of Chios 154, 155, 164, 180
Sky Captain and the World of Tomorrow 121
Sleeping Beauty 65
Socrates 155, 156
Sophocles 170, 177
Soul 6, 196, 198
Spielberg, Steven 30
Spirit in Man, Art, and Literature, The 62, 75
Star Wars 97
stellation 36, 37, 39
Stein, Murray 75, 102, 104, 106, 120, 196, 197
Storyland 93, 112, 121
storyline 7, 17, 26, 29, 31, 32, 33, 44, 50, 69, 143, 158, 160, 162, 169, 177
storytelling iv, 6, 7, 9, 10, 13, 14, 24, 30, 32, 33, 34, 39, 45, 47, 51, 53, 54, 61, 67, 69, 71, 78, 81, 87, 88, 89, 90, 91, 92, 97, 103, 116, 117, 124, 132, 133, 134, 168, 176
sub-plot 68
sub-plot pentagon 68
symbol 22, 32, 33, 34, 36, 38, 44, 47, 48, 51, 52, 55, 71, 72, 77, 78, 96, 161
Symposium 156

T

Technique of the Drama 40, 195
Tempest, The 139, 177
Thamus, King of Egypt 156
theme 7, 23, 24, 25, 26, 31, 32, 38, 39, 65, 83, 92, 93, 94, 95
Theory of Relativity 6
Theseus 105
Timaeus, The 71
Titanic 30, 31, 97
Tolkien, J. R. R. 25
Toy Story 18, 19

Index

Transcendent Function iv, 86, 87, 89, 90, 91, 96, 97, 98, 125, 129, 147, 148, 175, 197
Tutankhamen 44

U

Unconscious iv, vii, 45, 56, 57, 58, 59, 61, 63, 64, 65, 66, 75, 77, 78, 80, 81, 84, 85, 86, 87, 88, 89, 90, 96, 98, 99, 102, 103, 104, 105, 106, 107, 109, 110, 111, 112, 115, 116, 117, 118, 120, 122, 123, 124, 125, 126, 127, 128, 129, 132, 133, 134, 137, 139, 142, 146, 147, 148, 153, 161, 168, 172, 175, 178, 196
uroboros (see ouroboros)

V

Vampire vii, 19, 46, 64, 146, 169, 171, 173, 174, 175, 177, 197
van Franz, Marie Louise 64
Vitruvian Man 49

W

Walter, Richard 7, 16, 17, 18, 21, 64
Watcher at the Gates of Dawn, The 120
Watson, Emma 17
Wood, Dr. Renate 59, 170
World of Dreams 105, 130, 133
wormhole 39
Worthy vii, 80
Writing for Story 28

X

Xanadu 144

Y

Yantra 48, 56, 197
Yantra, The Tantric Symbol of Cosmic Unity 48, 197
yin-yang 22, 34, 35
Yoda 97

Z

Zodiac 32, 71

www.ingramcontent.com/pod-product-compliance
Lightning Source LLC
Chambersburg PA
CBHW031546040426
42452CB00006B/203